Santa Fe Railway

STEVE GLISCHINSKI

Motorbooks International
Publishers & Wholesalers

First published in 1997 by Motorbooks International Publishers & Wholesalers, PO Box 2, 729 Prospect Avenue, Osceola, WI 54020 USA

Library of Congress Cataloging-in-Publication Data Available
ISBN 0-7603-0380-0

Book editing, design and layout—Mike Schafer and Marshall Beecher/Andover Junction Publications

COVER: Until merged out of existence at the end of 1996, the Atchison, Topeka & Santa Fe Railway was always associated with quality service provided by state-of-the-art equipment such as this modern General Electric locomotive bearing the road's long-familiar red-and-silver colors. *Brian Solomon*

FRONTISPIECE: Detail of a new Electro-Motive diesel illustrates an unmistakable icon of the Santa Fe since 1937: the famous warbonnet paint-scheme design. *Brian Solomon*

TITLE PAGE: Hail to the *Chief!* Dawn sunlight bathes the profile of Santa Fe's eastbound *Chief* approaching Joliet (Illinois) Union Station on the last leg of its 2,235-mile journey between Los Angeles and Chicago in the spring of 1968. *Mike Schafer*

BACK COVER: Santa Fe passenger diesels rest at the 18th Street engine terminal in Chicago between their cross-country assignments in 1965. In the post-World War II years, there was hardly a boy who didn't yearn for (and better yet, receive) an electric train set with locomotives bearing the familiar colors of the Atchison, Topeka & Santa Fe. *Jim Boyd*

Santa Fe maintained a high profile in Western railroading right up to its merger with Burlington Northern on the eve of 1997. In the desert heat of a summer day in 1996, a blue-and-yellow AT&SF General Electric locomotive hustles along the main line at Goffs, California, with a high-speed intermodal train. *Marshall Beecher*

Printed in Hong Kong through World Print, Ltd.

Table of Contents

Acknowledgments

Generations of Americans grew up with the Santa Fe, either directly (as three-year-old Sam Smedley is doing near Edelstein, Illinois, in May 1996), or vicariously through books, movies, and videos featuring the AT&SF and electric trains painted in Santa Fe's familiar paint schemes. The Santa Fe Railway was a way of life in America for close to 140 years. *Steve Smedley*

Several individuals assisted in assembling this volume. Thanks must first go to Mike Schafer and Steve Esposito of Andover Junction Publications, who first brought the project to my attention and encouraged and supported my efforts. Mike's editing and design ability is second to none, and Steve's travels to the Railroad Museum of Pennsylvania—to which I also give thanks—to unearth photos is another example of their fine teamwork on the project. An old friend, Bud Bulgrin, opened his large Santa Fe library to me and provided full access to his huge collection of Santa Fe photographs and slides. Many thanks must also go to the numerous photographers who allowed their work to be reproduced on these pages. Without their efforts, much of the richness and color that was the Santa Fe would have slipped into history.

Two former Santa Fe employees deserve special recognition. Former Santa Fe president Michael R. Haverty, now president of Kansas City Southern Railway, was very gracious in allowing me to spend time with him for an article on the KCS for *Trains* Magazine, during which time we discussed his years on the Santa Fe. As the man responsible for bringing back the warbonnet paint scheme and capturing J. B. Hunt intermodal business, Mr. Haverty's contributions to Santa Fe in its final years were considerable. A special acknowledgment must go to Joe McMillan. Joe was employed for many years by the Santa Fe and has devoted his considerable photographic and journalistic skills to preserving the railway. He is the author of no less than five quality books on the AT&SF. As a Santa Fe expert, Joe happily agreed to review the manuscript and made many helpful and constructive suggestions. Thanks, Joe!

Finally, thanks to the team at Motorbooks International, who have supported the project from the beginning.

Steve Glischinski
Shoreview, Minnesota

When I was 15 years old in 1972, I saw my first Santa Fe train—sort of. Actually it was an Amtrak train, one of the *San Diegans*, pulling into the Santa Fe station at Fullerton, California. Although technically an Amtrak train, the consist was entirely Santa Fe, with warbonnet-painted F-units trailing fluted-sided, stainless-steel passenger cars. It rushed into the station, loaded a substantial number of passengers, and was gone in what seemed like a flash. My uncle, who knew I loved trains and had brought me to the depot, was a retired veteran of the Marine Corps who appreciated efficiency. The look on his face revealed he was mighty impressed by the Marine-like productivity of Santa Fe operations. I was as well, and that day on the Fullerton platform was the beginning of years of admiration for the Atchison, Topeka & Santa Fe Railway.

Santa Fe has always been one of the most famous and colorful railroads in North America. It carefully nurtured a positive public image, one that lives on in photographs, on model railroads, and in the pages of an incredible number of books and periodicals that have been published about the railway. This book is a modest contribution to the reams of literature on one of America's favorite railroads. It is part of Motorbooks International's new Railroad Color History Series and is intended not to be the ultimate history of the Santa Fe, but a handy reference source and historical overview for those interested in railroads in general and the AT&SF in particular, be they historians or just armchair readers. The book provides a broad view of how the vast Santa Fe system developed and grew, while providing readers with a feel for the life and times of the Santa Fe.

Since many readers find locomotives to be their main area of interest, there is expanded coverage of Santa Fe's motive-power fleet, both steam and diesel. Few would deny the beauty and power of Santa Fe steam, and, of course, its red and silver warbonnet paint scheme made its diesels both beautiful and popular among railroad fans and the general public. Santa Fe's wonderful fleet of passenger trains, including the famous *Super Chief* are included in these pages as well.

This book is by no means the last word on the Santa Fe. If it has simply whetted your appetite for more, then you can explore some of the numerous Santa Fe books, magazines, and other publications, or become a member of the Santa Fe Railway Historical & Modeling Society, which produces its own publication, *The Warbonnet*. Long after the last locomotive is repainted for the Burlington Northern & Santa Fe Railway, the enthusiasm of Santa Fe aficionados will carry on the memory of the Atchison, Topeka & Santa Fe Railway through these publications and organizations.

The Santa Fe map from a 1967 public timetable shows the system at nearly its full glory. Although some line retrenchments had occurred, particularly during the Depression era, this was the traditional network until the rationalization years of the 1970s-1980s.

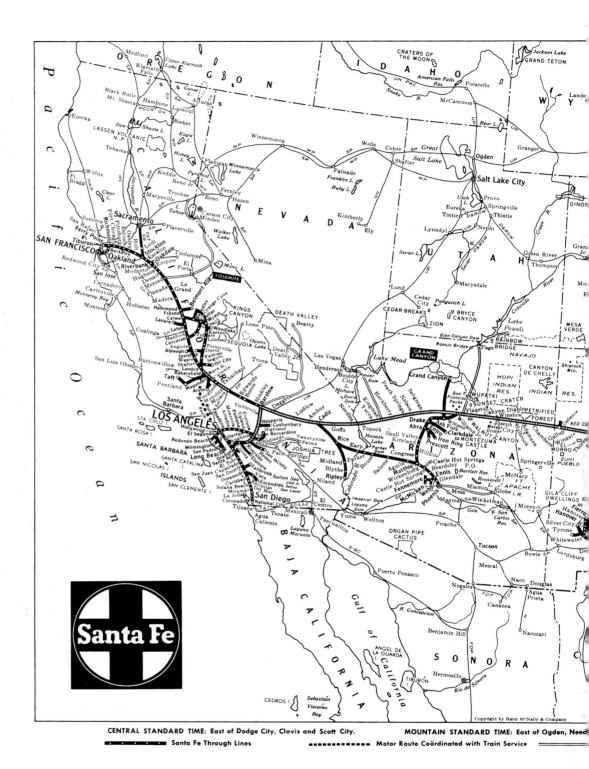

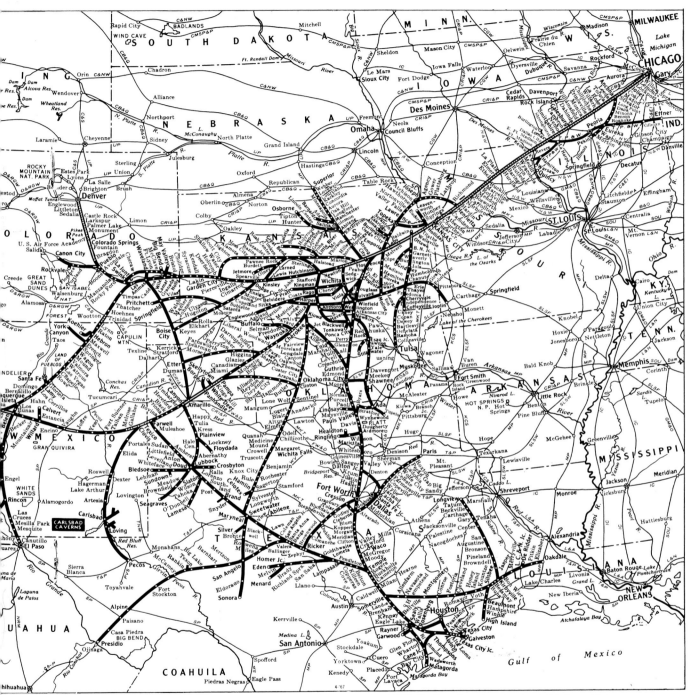

West of Dodge City and Clovis, and points Scott City to Garden City.

▭▭▭▭▭▭ Two Tracks

PACIFIC STANDARD TIME: Needles and west thereof, and west of Ogden and Parker.

MILEAGE OF LINES OPERATED .... 12,921 miles

Electro-Motive locomotives at Argentine Yard at Kansas City, Kansas, in 1966 reflect the two main facets of the Santa Fe—that catering to passengers (warbonnetted E8M No. 83) and that serving freight customers (blue-clad F7A 261). *Jim Boyd*

Santa Fe and Its Origins

1868–1900

Chances are, if you live in the United States, you've been touched in some way by the Atchison, Topeka & Santa Fe Railway—the legendary Santa Fe. Maybe it was the first time you heard the bouncy tune, "The Atchison, Topeka & the Santa Fe," composed by Johnny Mercer in 1945 for the hit film "The Harvey Girls," which chronicled the colorful women who served the patrons in Santa Fe's Harvey House restaurants. Perhaps you received a train set with a Santa Fe locomotive painted in the famous red-and-silver "warbonnet" colors. Or, if you were really lucky, you were treated to a ride aboard one of Santa Fe's famous streamliners across the American West.

The Santa Fe holds a special place in American railroad lore. It had a long and colorful history, which began in 1868 when the first spade of earth was turned to start construction in Topeka, Kansas, and ended on December 31, 1996, when the company was officially merged with Burlington Northern Railroad to form the Burlington Northern & Santa Fe Railway (BNSF). What happened in between those two dates is the subject of this history.

Building Along the Legendary Santa Fe Trail

On April 3, 1826, Cyrus K. Holliday was born near Carlisle, Pennsylvania. He made his fortune in railroad construction, and in 1854 moved west to the plains of Kansas. Shortly after his arrival, he participated in the development of the city of Topeka, along the Kansas River about 50 miles west of the Missouri border. Like most towns in the nineteenth century American West, a railroad was deemed to be an essential ingredient if Topeka was to prosper. Access to a railroad offered towns reliable, speedy transportation for both people and goods, and with it the opportunity to grow and prosper. Holliday hoped a new railroad would attract more settlers to the plains of the Midwest that bordered the famed Santa Fe Trail, which stretched from the Missouri River to Santa Fe, in northern New Mexico. Already, Kansas was growing: between 1855 and 1861 the population of Kansas soared from 8,500 to 143,000.

Santa Fe had been established in 1610 as the seat of the Spanish colony of New Mexico. Trade between the United States and New Mexico began in 1822, after Mexico gained its independence from Spain. To further this trade, the Santa Fe Trail was established between Independence, Missouri, just east of Kansas City, and Santa Fe. It wound across Kansas following the divide between the Kansas (Kaw) and Arkansas rivers to what is now Great Bend, Kansas, then followed the Arkansas west to present day La Junta, Colorado. From La Junta, the Trail climbed over Raton Pass into New Mexico, then followed the Canadian River through present day Las Vegas, New Mexico. At that point it turned west and crossed the Sangre de Cristo Mountains through Glorietta Pass and into Santa Fe. In 1866 R. L. Wooten opened a toll road over Raton Pass for travelers; he would play an important role when the Santa Fe Railroad came to Raton twelve years later. In 1848, after war with Mexico, Santa Fe and New Mexico came

The Santa Fe was born in Topeka, and for years the Kansas capital was the heart of the railroad. In this 1874 view at the Topeka depot, engine No. 5, the *Thomas Sherlock*, has very important cargo in tow— employee wages in the pay car. The 4-4-0 locomotive was built in 1870 by Taunton Locomotive Works for $5,800.and served until 1911. *Railroad Museum of Pennsylvania*

under U.S. control, offering more incentive for a railroad to link the isolated New Mexicans with the rest of the U.S.

In 1859, a charter was granted by the Kansas legislature to build the Atchison & Topeka Railroad. According to the charter, the northern end of the railroad was to rest on the north bank of the Missouri River opposite St. Joseph, Missouri, while the other end of the line would be at Topeka. It was September 1860 before Holliday and a dozen other men raised some preliminary capital and formally organized the railroad at a meeting in a small brick law office in Atchison, Kansas.

Nothing came of the plan for the next four years when Holliday and Senator S. C. Pomeroy pushed land-grant legislation through Congress, which was signed by President Lincoln on March 3, 1863. The legislation provided for a land grant of three million acres along the proposed route from Atchison to Topeka "to the western line of the State [of Kansas] in the direction of Fort Union and Santa Fe." To obtain the grant, the rail line had to be completed to the Colorado border by December 31, 1872. On November 24, 1863, the company changed its name to the Atchison, Topeka & Santa Fe Railroad, which added the colorful name of

the Santa Fe Trail to the venture.

For the next four years Holliday and his partners attempted to raise cash for the company with little success. In 1868, Congress came to the rescue: it authorized the AT&SF to purchase unalloted lands of the Pottawattomie Indian Reservation near Topeka for $1 an acre. The company then resold the land to farmers, which provided the necessary funds to start construction. On October 30, 1868, construction finally began in Topeka on Washington Street, between Fourth and Fifth Street.

On March 30, 1869 a bridge over the Kaw (Kansas) River was completed which allowed a connection with the Kansas Pacific (now part of Union Pacific). This allowed construction materials to reach the railroad freely and hastened the building. On April 26, 1869, Santa Fe's first locomotive, named *Cyrus K. Holliday*, pulled its first train, a two-car excursion special filled with invited guests. The crew of this first Santa Fe train consisted of engineer George Beach, fireman Brit Craft, conductor W. W. Fagen, and brakemen Bill Bartling and Al Dugan. They ran the train over seven miles of line from Topeka west to Wakarusa where the passengers climbed into carriages for the trip to the Wakarusa picnic grounds; the rail line was only completed for seven miles, but the picnic ground was twelve miles away! Nonetheless, Holliday gave a speech at the celebration where he predicted the Santa Fe would one day be a giant system, reaching Chicago, St. Louis, Galveston, San Francisco, and Mexico City. Holliday proved to be prophetic indeed: most of his predictions would, in time, come true—and with Holliday living to see most of his dream become reality.

Financial control of the company shifted to Boston, Massachusetts, in 1869 as construction crews continued the Santa Fe's push west after the opening celebration. By July 1871 the railroad was complete to Newton, Kansas, 137 miles from Topeka, and on May 16, 1872, the line was opened from Topeka east to Atchison, which gave the Santa Fe connections to other railroads and points east. Also that month, a Santa Fe affiliate, the Wichita & Southwestern, completed a line from Newton to Wichita.

However, to receive its land grant, construction would have to reach the Kansas border by the end of 1872—and the border was still 300 miles from Newton. At a cost of $5 million, crews worked frantically to reach the Colorado line. They reached Dodge City, 153 miles from Newton, on September 19 and kept on going toward the unmarked border. Three months later, on December 22, the "border" was reached and the celebrations began. But as the construction crews celebrated, federal surveyors examined their work and pronounced that the railroad was still four miles short of the real border! Workers pulled up rail and ties from sidings and threw it down on a hastily built right-of-way, and on December 28 the border was reached. The Santa Fe had its land grant. But this was only the beginning of what would soon become a vast rail system.

Established in 1610, Santa Fe, New Mexico, was an important point on the Santa Fe Trail and is one of the oldest settlements in America. Interestingly, the AT&SF main line bypassed Santa Fe, which instead was served by a branch off the main line at Lamy, New Mexico. The railroad operated this adobe-style ticket office in Santa Fe and shuttled passengers to and from Lamy in jitneys, one of which stands at left in this scene from the 1920s. *Railroad Museum of Pennsylvania*

ABOVE: A connecting stage awaits the arrival of a Santa Fe express train wheeling into Burlingame, Kansas, around the turn of the century. *Railroad Museum of Pennsylvania*

The railroad reached Newton, Kansas, in 1871. At the time of this photo—probably not long after the Santa Fe arrived—it appears that the depot had become the social center of town. *Railroad Museum of Pennsylvania*

Expansion Under W. B. Strong

In 1875, the Santa Fe reached Kansas City by leasing several short lines (small railroads not affiliated with a large carrier) which were later were merged into the system. On the western front, expansion continued as the company pushed west into Colorado. Santa Fe affiliate Pueblo & Arkansas Valley built west along the Arkansas River, completing the line from the Kansas border to Pueblo, Colorado, on February 29, 1876. The following year

William Barstow Strong became Santa Fe's general manager. He pursued an aggressive agenda of railroad construction, and more than any other was the man was responsible for making Holliday's vision reality. He became Santa Fe's president in 1881.

With Strong pushing for expansion, the company was again on the move. To reach Santa Fe, the company built south from Pueblo toward New Mexico. Another railroad, the narrow gauge Denver & Rio

ABOVE: The combined westbound *El Capitan/Super Chief* is at Wooten, Colorado, well into its grinding climb toward Raton Pass on September 13, 1969. Nearly a century earlier as the Santa Fe was making its westward push, Raton was seen as the logical route into New Mexico from southeastern Colorado. Since construction of the line over Raton, this crossing of the lower Rocky Mountain range has been a scenic highlight for passengers, but it was an operational headache for the railroad. Today it is a secondary route, with most east-west freight traffic bypassing Raton via the Belen Cutoff. *David W. Salter*

LEFT: A Denver-bound "Q" ("Quality" series) train sweeps along the "Joint Line" at Palmer Lake, Colorado, in 1987. One hundred years earlier, Santa Fe attained its own line into Denver via subsidiary Denver & Santa Fe Railway. Eventually, AT&SF and Denver & Rio Grande Western began joint operations of the rail corridor from the south into Denver, hence the Joint Line title. *Tom Hoffmann*

At 7,421 feet above sea level, Glorieta, New Mexico, near Santa Fe, would be the highest point on the entire railroad. The station at Glorieta is shown in 1938. The approaching passenger train is carrying one of the many new lightweight streamlined cars being delivered to the railroad that year. *Railroad Museum of Pennsylvania*

Grande Railway, was also building south toward El Paso, Texas. Rio Grande rails reached south to El Moro, near Trinidad on the Colorado-New Mexico border. The logical choice for both roads to gain entrance to New Mexico was over Raton Pass. Since there was only room for one line over the Pass, the first road to begin construction would be the winner of the contest.

On February 26, 1878, civil engineers of both lines rode a Rio Grande train to El Moro. Neither was aware that the other was on board the train. Upon arrival, the Rio Grande crew went to their hotel for the night, but the Santa Fe crew went right to work. Strong had ordered Santa Fe chief engineer A. A. Robinson to occupy and hold the pass. Robinson approached R. L. Wooten and secured an agreement with him to build over the pass. Just hours later, on February 27, the Rio Grande crews came to work, and discovered the

Santa Fe engineers had already laid claim to Raton Pass. On December 7, 1878 the first Santa Fe train operated over Raton and entered New Mexico, using a hastily built line which included "switchbacks"— short tracks on which trains could move back and forth to gain elevation. These tracks were eliminated when a new tunnel was opened on September 1, 1879. However, steep grades remained which would have Santa Fe thinking of ways to bypass Raton Pass after the turn of the century.

Just a month after the Raton Pass incident, another Santa Fe/Rio Grande conflict broke out, this time over the right to pass through Colorado's Royal Gorge. A short time after Santa Fe arrived in Pueblo in 1876, a silver rush was breaking out at Leadville, 150 miles to the northwest in the Colorado Rockies. Santa Fe decided to it needed to serve the Leadville mines, but this would require negotiating the narrow Royal Gorge of the Colorado River west of

CHAPTER 1

The Santa Fe reached Albuquerque, New Mexico, in 1880. As the state's largest city, Albuquerque became one of the most important points along the Santa Fe main line between Chicago and Los Angeles. An overview of the city's station area shows Santa Fe's classic mission-style depot as the Chicago-bound *Grand Canyon* makes its passenger stop on January 12, 1968. *Bud Bulgrin*

Canon City. The Denver & Rio Grande also intended to build from Pueblo to Leadville through the Gorge. Gangs hired by the two railroads threatened one another and carried small arms. Soon the story of a Royal Gorge "war" was sensationalized by tabloids of the day.

For a time, Santa Fe workers seized the Gorge, but the Supreme Court ruled that the Rio Grande had prior rights to build through it, with use to be shared by both railroads. The Royal Gorge conflict came to an end when the two lines came to an agreement on February 2, 1880. Santa Fe dropped the idea of a Leadville extension and let Rio Grande have the Gorge, and Rio Grande gave up its goal of reaching El Paso. Rio Grande permitted Santa Fe to lay a third (standard gauge) rail on its narrow-gauge line between Pueblo and Denver in 1882 giving Santa Fe its first access to the latter city. However, in

1887, when the Missouri Pacific reached Pueblo, giving Rio Grande a new outlet to the east, Santa Fe subsidiary Denver & Santa Fe Railway built its own line from Pueblo into Denver. Later the two roads coordinated their operations from Trinidad to Denver, forming what became known as the "Joint Line" and today a busy rail corridor.

BELOW: At the turn of the century, folks entertained themselves looking at stereoscopic scenes such as this of a Santa Fe train crossing Cañon Diablo in 1903. *Railroad Museum of Pennsylvania*

From Raton, construction crews headed through scenic Glorieta Pass and toward Santa Fe. In January 1879 chief engineer Robinson recommended to Strong that the main line not enter Santa Fe proper due to difficult terrain. Instead the railroad built an 18-mile branch line from Lamy, New Mexico, into Santa Fe, which was completed on February 16, 1880. Two months later the railroad reached Albuquerque. Throughout the 1880s the railroad added many branch lines in Kansas to serve the rich "wheat country."

Having reached New Mexico, the railroad set its sights on further expansion, notably west to California, south into Mexico, and east to Chicago, which would become the nation's railroad capital and corporate headquarters for the Santa Fe.

In January 1880, Santa Fe acquired half of the Atlantic & Pacific Company (A&P), which was also fifty percent owned by the St. Louis & San Francisco Railway (Frisco). The A&P had been created by an act of Congress in 1866 to build from Springfield, Missouri, to the Pacific Ocean, including a land grant. By 1876 it had constructed 293 miles of line, all in Missouri, but the company defaulted on interest payments and was sold to the Frisco in 1879. The following year the Santa Fe and Frisco revived

the railroad, and construction was begun on the western division of the A&P from New Mexico to California. By the end of 1880 the A&P had constructed 75 miles of track west from Isleta, south of Albuquerque, toward the New Mexico/Arizona border. The principal locomotive shop for the A&P was established at Albuquerque.

Watching all this activity with more than passing interest was the Southern Pacific (SP), which had constructed an iron lariat of lines through California, and also reached north to Oregon and east to Texas. The SP essentially controlled railroad activity in California and viewed Santa Fe's potential entry into the state with anxiety. At the time, SP was controlled by Collis P. Huntington and financier Jay Gould. To stop the A&P, SP forces built a new line from Mojave to Needles, California, beating A&P to the town and essentially blocking its access to the state. A&P construction continued across Arizona, reaching the Colorado River south of Needles, where construction began on a new railroad bridge. The two roads linked up in Needles on July 12, 1883, but Santa Fe had little reason for celebration since SP refused to develop traffic via the new connection. This was also partly due to the fact SP already had a route to the Pacific via Deming, New

Santa Fe's main line crosses the Colorado River—and the California border—at Topock, Arizona. This westbound is about to cross the state line in March 1996. *Steve Glischinski*

Santa Fe's large, rambling depot and divisional headquarters building at San Bernardino is shown in 1923. "San Berdoo" became Santa Fe's main yard and shop facility in the Los Angeles basin. *Railroad Museum of Pennsylvania*

Gateway to the Los Angeles basin was and is Cajon Pass for all three major players in Southern California railroading: Santa Fe, Union Pacific, and Southern Pacific, although SP was a latecomer (mid-1960s) to using Cajon. In July 1969, a westbound Santa Fe freight slinks downhill from Summit, California. Leading the quintet of locomotives is an Alco DL-series diesel—an "Alligator" to the many train-watchers that haunt Cajon. *Mike Schafer*

With downtown Chicago as a backdrop, westbound train 123, the *Grand Canyon*, sets out for the West Coast on a late summer morning in 1961. The Santa Fe did not reach Chicago until 1888, but doing so greatly elevated the company's prominence in the railroad industry; for many years AT&SF was the only single-line carrier between Chicago and California. *Richard J. Solomon*

Mexico. This was longer than the A&P's by 232 miles, and SP had no reason to "short haul" itself by routing business via the A&P. While the two roads did reach an agreement to favor the Needles route for passenger service, freight business remained disappointing.

But Santa Fe had other tricks up its sleeve, notably a route into Mexico. The railroad established the Sonora Railway to build from the Gulf of Mexico port of Guaymas to Nogales on the Arizona border, which was completed in 1879. The company received a land grant of 15,000 acres per mile from the Mexican government, a grant which the SP had hoped to receive. At Nogales, the railroad connected with the New Mexico & Arizona, a subsidiary of the Santa Fe. The New Mexico & Arizona used a portion of the Southern Pacific between Deming, New Mexico, and Benson, Arizona, to connect with the newly built line from Albuquerque to Rincon and Deming (another new line extended from Rincon to El Paso, Texas). Santa Fe then had a 1,700-mile route from Kansas City to the Pacific Ocean at Guaymas.

Despite SP's blocking maneuvers, in October 1880 the California Southern Railroad was organized to build from San Diego through San Bernardino, California, to meet the A&P. By 1883 the line had opened to San Bernardino (after fighting with SP for the right to cross its line at Colton), and the first passenger train was welcomed on September 13. Meanwhile, President Strong negotiated with SP's Huntington for the purchase of the Needles-Mojave line. By then Huntington had overextended his fortune and was willing to negotiate. In 1884 Huntington and Gould sold their interest in the Frisco and entered into a temporary lease of the Needles-Mojave line at a high price. Santa Fe also received rights to use SP tracks between Mojave and San Francisco, also at high rates.

To complete the line, California Southern would need to close the gap between San Bernardino and Barstow, the connection with the Needles-Mojave line. To do so would require building over Cajon Pass. This pass is a gap between the San Bernardino and San Gabriel mountains northeast of Los Angeles, along the famous

CHAPTER 1

San Andreas Fault. Construction on the line between San Bernardino and Barstow via Cajon was completed in November 1885. The grades over Cajon were steep, because of the great change in elevation: San Bernardino is 1,077 feet above sea level, and the summit of the pass, about 25 miles east, is at 3,823 feet. Because of the steep grades, a second track was opened in 1912. Though two miles longer, the second track has less steep grades. In 1905, Union Pacific trains began using Santa Fe's tracks over the pass as well. Because it was busy, employed large steam power, and trains frequently employed "helper" engines (additional locomotives added to assist trains over grades) Cajon became one of the most popular train-watching locations in the U.S. for railroad fans.

Meanwhile the route into San Diego had its problems. The San Diego line utilized rugged Temecula Canyon northeast of Oceanside to reach San Bernardino. This route was prone to flooding during the rainy season, so in 1888 a new line was built along the California coast between Los Angeles and Oceanside. Dubbed the "Surf Line" due to its close proximity to the Pacific Ocean (in some cases the railroad goes right down the beach), after its completion the line via Temecula Canyon was abandoned.

Santa Fe received rights over SP rails between Colton, just outside San Bernardino, to Los Angeles in 1885, but two years later Santa Fe extended its own line into Los Angeles from San Bernardino via Pasadena. This became the main line for passenger trains serving the city, while another line from San Bernardino through Riverside into Los Angeles opened August 12, 1888, and became the primary freight route into L.A. The Pasadena line was sold in 1994 to the Southern California Regional Rail Authority for use as a light-rail mass-transit line. Today both freight and Amtrak passenger trains utilize the route via Riverside into Los Angeles. With San Bernardino becoming a strategic junction point for Santa Fe in southern California, huge locomotive shops were constructed there. At one time they were the second largest locomotive shops in the country. Only the Pennsylvania Railroad shops in Altoona, Pennsylvania, were larger. The San Bernardino Shops remained in operation until 1992.

The mention of Santa Fe often conjures up images of mainline railroading, but the carrier once fielded an extensive network of branchlines in Kansas, Oklahoma, and Texas which tapped countless backwater burghs whose existence depended on agriculture—and they depended on the Santa Fe for ag transportation. This scene at Carmen, Oklahoma, is on the "Orient" line. *Paul Enenbach*

One of the final main routes completed by the Santa Fe was up California's Central Valley to the San Francisco Bay Area. As a through route, the line began operation in 1900. Easily the route's most notable segment was the climb over the Tehachapi Mountains in Southern California, which Santa Fe operated over via trackage rights on the Southern Pacific between Mojave and Bakersfield, California. In June 1964, a trio of Electro-Motive SD24 diesels round Tehachapi Loop during their trip over the mountains. *Bud Bulgrin*

Expansion wasn't limited to the west end of the system. Santa Fe reached Chicago in 1888 after a rapid construction project by subsidiary Chicago, Santa Fe & California Railway, which was formed to construct the line from Kansas City to Chicago. This company built 350 miles of new track from Kansas City to Ancona, Illinois, where it met the tracks of the Chicago & St. Louis Railway, which had built a line from Chicago to Pekin (across and down the Illinois River from Peoria) hoping to reach St. Louis. This railroad was purchased, and after it was rehabilitated, the Chicago-Ancona portion became part of Santa Fe's Kansas City-Chicago route. Because of the direct nature of the route between the two cities, the Kansas City-Chicago route became known as the "air line." In 1891 Santa Fe trains began using Dearborn Station in Chicago, which would be "home base" for the company's passenger trains for the next 80 years.

The mid-1880s also saw President Strong thinking about expanding the system to the Gulf of Mexico. The Missouri Pacific, also controlled by Jay Gould, held a position of strength in Gulf and Texas markets, but Strong felt Santa Fe could compete and be a player moving traffic between the Midwest and the Gulf. Its avenue into Texas would be the Gulf, Colorado & Santa Fe Railway. Chartered in 1873 by citizens of Galveston, Texas, and at the time not affiliated with the Santa Fe, the GC&SF was organized to build from Galveston to Santa Fe. Construction started in 1875, but in three years the company had made it only 60 miles out of Galveston and was on the edge of financial collapse. Purchased by entrepreneur George Sealy, the company was revitalized and by 1882 reached Houston, Dallas, and Fort Worth. Catching the attention of Strong, he and Sealy entered into negotiations for Santa Fe to purchase the GC&SF. The two came

to agreement in 1886, after hard bargaining: in exchange for control of GC&SF, Strong insisted the railroad construct 375 miles of new track over the next year. Sealy agreed, and then Strong offered to finance the construction. GC&SF crews worked furiously over the next year to build the new trackage, pushing north into Indian territory in Oklahoma. Santa Fe built south from Arkansas City, Kansas, and the two met at Purcell, Oklahoma, in 1887. Santa Fe now had its Texas entry, and over the years expanded its holdings to cover the state.

Closing Out the Century

By 1889, Santa Fe had built a network of lines of 8,118 miles, including trackage jointly owned with other railroads. Its routes reached Chicago, Galveston, Los Angeles, and San Diego. But as other railroads invaded Santa Fe territory, its strength diminished. Economic conditions worsened, and banks which held Santa Fe's bonds forced President Strong to leave the presidency. Many blamed Strong for building too rapidly, but in the future the strength of the Santa Fe system would vindicate his vision. With tight reins on credit and the railroads fortunes declining, the railroad entered bankruptcy in 1893. In 1895, a new company, the Atchison, Topeka & Santa Fe Railway, was incorporated which purchased Santa Fe's assets out of receivership, and Edward P. Ripley was named president. Ripley was conservative and careful in making expenditures. Eventually he could claim that Santa Fe had the lowest funded debt per mile of any major railroad.

Ripley went to work to tighten up the vast system. Small unprofitable lines were abandoned, and holdings in the Frisco, which had been acquired in 1890, were sold. The company assumed full control of the vital Atlantic & Pacific line across New Mexico and Arizona from the Frisco. Knowing SP greatly valued access to Mexico, in 1897 the two railroads worked out a deal to trade the Sonora Railway and the Benson-Nogales line to the SP in exchange for ownership of SP's Needles-Mojave line. In hindsight this trade proved to be brilliant—at least as far as Santa Fe was concerned—since the Mexican lines ultimately were not nearly as valuable for SP as the California lines were for AT&SF. Ripley also approved an overhaul of the main line between Chicago and Los Angeles, including relocation projects which shortened the route by 50 miles.

In 1898 Santa Fe expanded further into SP's California empire. The San Francisco & San Joaquin Valley Railroad completed a 234-mile line from Bakersfield to Stockton on May 27, and Santa Fe acquired the road later the same year to gain control of its own route through the San Joaquin Valley. To connect the new railroad with the rest of its system, in 1899 Santa Fe obtained rights to operate over SP tracks between Mojave and Bakersfield over the rugged Tehachapi Mountains, including the world famous "Tehachapi Loop" at Walong, California. This engineering marvel was constructed by SP in a two-year project completed in 1876. Laid out by SP assistant chief engineer William Hood to conquer steep grades in a minimum of distance, the line makes a complete circle, crossing over itself at the same time gaining 77 feet in elevation. The loop was an unusual construction technique in railroading and even today crowds of onlookers gather to watch trains traverse it.

To finish the route to the San Francisco Bay area, the railroad began construction of a 71-mile line from Stockton to Richmond, California, on San Francisco Bay. The rugged route passed through swampland and required the building of five tunnels through the coastal mountains, including the longest on the system, the 5,596-foot Franklin Tunnel at Glen Frazer. The new route opened in 1900. Santa Fe also began ferry service across San Francisco Bay from Richmond to China Basin in San Francisco, and built up its own "navy" of ferries, tugboats, and barges to make the crossing. In 1904 through the purchase and rebuilding of another railroad, Santa Fe acquired its own route from Richmond into Oakland.

Now Santa Fe had control of its own routes from Chicago to Los Angeles, San Diego, the Bay Area and into the heart of Texas. No other railroad could make the same claim. The vision of Cyrus K. Holliday, who remained a Santa Fe director until his death in 1900, had been fulfilled. In the new twentieth century, more expansion and improvements were to come.

One of Santa Fe's most important accomplishments of the early twentieth century was the construction of the Belen Cutoff through east-central New Mexico. The new line provided a low-grade alternate route for Chicago-California traffic as well as an artery for traffic out of Texas. The Cutoff's most scenic landmark is Abo Canyon at the west end of the line. In October 1992, an eastbound Santa Fe freight snakes into the canyon behind a pair of EMD diesels wearing the "yellow bonnet" livery. *Steve Glischinski*

Into the Twentieth Century

1900-1930

As Santa Fe entered the twentieth century under the leadership of E. P. Ripley, the company continued to enhance and improve its physical plant and services. While William Barstow Strong had concentrated on rapid expansion of the system, Ripley proceeded more cautiously. He added new trackage only if traffic (and profitability) warranted, but new equipment was continually acquired. For example, in 1900, 109 steam locomotives, 582 freight cars, and 12 passengers cars joined the roster. Orders for new locomotives and cars became a Santa Fe hallmark: the company continued the practice right into the 1990s.

An Emblem is Born

During the Ripley regime, one of the most famous and long-lasting symbols of the Santa Fe was born: the cross and circle emblem. The logo, which Santa Fe used as its corporate logo until merger into Burlington Northern & Santa Fe (which utilizes a variation of it), first came into use in 1901, but there are several stories as to its origin. One relates that J. J. Byrne, passenger traffic manager at Los Angeles at the time, was the person responsible for the emblem. Displeased with the logo in use then, it was said he called a meeting of his traffic representatives to brainstorm ideas for a new symbol. At the meeting, Byrne supposedly took out a silver dollar, drew a circle around the outside of it and drew a cross within it creating the cross and circle. Another story relates that Santa Fe officials came up with the design. Like Byrne, they used a silver dollar to form a circle, which was intended to symbolize the wheels of transportation. Inside the circle

they placed a cross, which had three meanings: (1) the four points of the compass; (2) the cross carried by the Franciscans during the Spanish expeditions in the Southwest; (3) and the pagan sign of the sun used by the Native Americans of the Southwest.

Still another story indicates the emblem was devised aboard a train by Santa Fe executives. They placed a cross on a poker chip, which was said to symbolize the cross and circle that Indians in New Mexico had used to symbolize Christian faith. The cross stood for the sun god the Indians had worshiped.

The Santa Fe, in its company publications, gave Byrne credit for the emblem, which they reported was designed by him aboard a train in February 1901—using a silver dollar to draw a circle surrounding a cross. Byrne was a student of the Southwest, and knew the various meanings the cross had to Indians and Spanish Christians who came to the Southwest. He drew the circle to represent transportation, put the cross in the middle of the circle and wrote SANTA FE, the railroad's nickname, through the cross. Santa Fe used the emblem both as a free-standing circle or sometimes placed the circle within a square. Both versions were official, and became one of the most enduring symbols of Western railroading, remaining in use for 95 years. Only the bar-and-ball emblem of the Chicago & North Western Railway was in use longer.

The Belen Cutoff

Much like James J. Hill of the Great Northern Railway in the Pacific Northwest, Santa Fe established early on a tradition of

ABOVE: Another product of Santa Fe's early twentieth century history was the road's famous cross-and-circle emblem, one of which adorns the depot at Edelstein, Illinois, as well as the nose of the Electro-Motive GP20 locomotive nearby. Both illustrate how the logo sometimes appeared within a square.
Jim Boyd

FACING PAGE: Perishable traffic dominates this westbound sweeping along the Belen Cutoff west of Willard, New Mexico, in 1974, behind three EMD and two Alco locomotives.
Mike Schafer

making line changes, adding signaling, and rebuilding its track structure. The goal was to lower the cost of railroad operations and improve service to customers — both passengers and shippers. One of the biggest improvements undertaken after the turn of the century was the Belen Cutoff.

Since the line through northern New Mexico to Santa Fe opened in 1880, the route over Raton and Glorieta passes had presented problems for the railroad. The line over Raton in particular was an operational headache. It had steep grades which greatly slowed trains and required the use of expensive-to-operate "helper" locomotives to push trains over the pass. With traffic on the increase, the route over Raton was improved after the turn of the century. Between 1901 and 1905 Santa Fe laid a second main track over the pass to ease congestion. The 1879-built tunnel at the summit of Raton was single track and too small to fit freight cars of the day, so a second, larger tunnel was constructed. The new tunnel paralleled the old and was longer—2,789-feet versus 2,041 feet—and

therefore had an easier grade. It was opened for service on July 9, 1908. The old tunnel stayed in service and was later enlarged, but was finally abandoned in 1953.

Despite the second track, the problem of Raton's steep grades remained. The track rose 1,661 feet in 16 miles over Raton, and 158 feet in one mile over Glorieta Pass. Trains over Raton still required helper locomotives. Even today, long Burlington Northern & Santa Fe coal trains must be broken into sections and assisted over the pass with helpers. To ease the bottleneck, Santa Fe looked into bypassing Raton altogether. The railroad decided to combine existing segments of its lines in Kansas, Oklahoma, and Texas with new construction to build a "cutoff" and bypass Raton.

Survey work began in 1902 under the supervision of Chief Engineer James Dun. Termed the Belen Cutoff, the new route required the construction of 250 miles of line from the Texas-New Mexico state line at Texico, Texas, to Belen, New Mexico. The line into Texico was built in 1898, and was

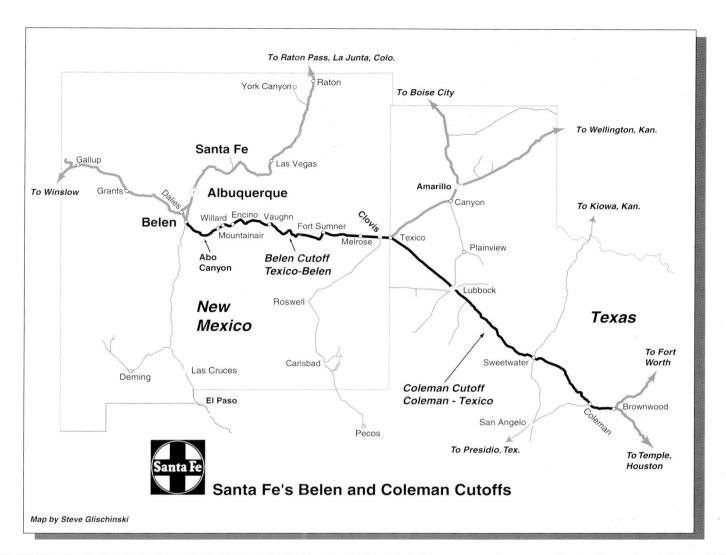

York Canyon ○ ○ Raton *To Raton Pass, La Junta, Colo.*

To Boise City

To Wellington, Kan.

Santa Fe

○ Las Vegas

Amarillo
○ Canyon

To Kiowa, Kan.

Gallup ○
Albuquerque

To Winslow   Grants ○   Dalies

Belen   Willard   Encino   Vaughn
Mountainair   Fort Sumner   **Clovis**
                  Melrose   Texico

Plainview ○

**Abo
Canyon**

***Belen Cutoff
Texico-Belen***

Lubbock ○

Roswell

***New
Mexico***

Texas

Carlsbad

*To Fort
Worth*

Sweetwater ○

Deming ○   Las Cruces

***Coleman Cutoff
Coleman - Texico***

Brownwood ○
Coleman

El Paso

San Angelo ○

Pecos ○

To Presidio, Tex.

*To Temple,
Houston*

Santa Fe

Santa Fe's Belen and Coleman Cutoffs

Map by Steve Glischinski

RIGHT: Most east-west Santa Fe through freights operated by way of Waynoka, Oklahoma, Amarillo, Texas, and the Belen Cutoff while most passenger runs used the original main line via Raton. However, one latter-day train of note, the *San Francisco Chief,* followed the freight route between Wellington, Kansas, and Dalies, New Mexico. Three Alco PA-type passenger diesels lead the westbound *S.F. Chief* at Clovis, in April 1967. *Tom Hoffmann*

Train QLA is in the midst of a crew change at the handsome Waynoka depot in May 1975. The QLA was a joint operation with the St. Louis-San Francisco Railway, which handled the train out of Tulsa west to Avard and Waynoka where it was handed over to Santa Fe crews. From here, the train becomes yet another entry in the fleet of east-west traffic moving between the Midwest and California. *Paul Enenbach*

part of another shortline acquisition by the growing Santa Fe. The Pecos Valley Railway had built a line north from Pecos, Texas, to Carlsbad and Roswell, New Mexico, but ran into financial difficulties. The line turned to AT&SF for help, and, aided by the Santa Fe, another line was set up— the Pecos Valley & Northeastern Railway. This company, which acquired the Pecos Valley Railway in 1898, was incorporated to build north from Roswell to Texico and into Amarillo, which was reached in April 1899. The "Pecos Valley" line eventually was absorbed by Santa Fe.

Construction on the Belen Cutoff began in January 1903, then stalled because of a scarcity of money until August 1905. The first train ran over the line on December 18, 1907, but it was not formally opened until July 1, 1908, when a ten-mile connection from Belen to the Raton Pass line at Dalies, New Mexico, was opened. At the east end of the Cutoff about ten miles west of Texico, Santa Fe created a new town, Clovis, to serve as a division point and built a shop and roundhouse (it remains a division point today). Another division point was located at Vaughn, New Mexico, about halfway across the Cutoff, where a large fill was built to cross over the tracks of the Rock Island. Tracks were laid through short, rugged Abo Canyon and into Belen, which became another new division point with a 17-stall concrete roundhouse built in 1907.

Trains were rerouted from the Raton

route through Wellington, Kansas, across the Texas Panhandle to Amarillo and on to Clovis, across New Mexico and into Belen. While the route from Chicago to Belen via the Cutoff was only six miles shorter than the line over Raton, the steep grades were avoided. The only substantial grades on the new route were 25 miles east of Belen, where the new line traversed scenic Abo Canyon. The elevation at Belen was 4,785 feet, while 41 miles east at Mountainair the elevation was 6,508 feet. This meant Santa Fe would have to contend with a 1.25 percent grade, but this was far better than the 3 to 3.5 percent grades found on Raton Pass. Abo Canyon itself is less than five miles long, but the line through it required the construction of seven concrete and steel bridges as the railroad crossed and recrossed the Abo River. Eastbound trains climbed the steep, curving grade between the west end of the canyon at Sais and the Abo summit at Mountainair. In steam and early diesel days, helpers were required to push trains between Belen and Mountainair, but these were eliminated with the advent of more powerful diesel locomotives.

The opening of the Belen Cutoff allowed Santa Fe to route most freight traffic south to the new line, but most passenger trains continued to use the northern route over Raton and Glorieta passes so that Denver connections could be maintained (at La Junta, Colorado) as well as service to southeastern Colorado and Albuquerque. Besides, passenger trains were less affected by the grades.

The Cutoff became and remains one of the busiest lines on the system. To handle the heavy traffic, Centralized Traffic Control (CTC) signaling was installed in 1943-44. The mainly single-track line received many miles of second main as Santa Fe expanded capacity across its main lines in the 1990s.

Even before the new route via Belen was opened, Santa Fe toyed with the idea of building another cutoff to bypass Raton Pass. It had originally been proposed prior to the construction of the line over Raton Pass; the route would have been far east of the line over Raton in desert country. The railroad originally decided against this route because of the sparse population. The route would have left the main line at Dodge City, Kansas, heading southwest,

linking up with the main line at Colmor, New Mexico. Eventually named the Colmor Cutoff, the entire route was surveyed in 1910, and in the 1920s and 1930s trackage was built to the town of Farley, New Mexico, only 35 miles from Colmor. However, even though the cutoff would be 69 miles shorter than the route over Raton, it would not have avoided the grades over Glorieta Pass. Farley remained the end-of-track, and with the Great Depression and resulting traffic declines the railroad decided against completing the route. The trackage from Farley to Boise City, Oklahoma, was pulled up in 1942 and the Colmor Cutoff became another of railroading's "what ifs?"

The Peavine, the A&C, and California Southern

Another shortcut route was developed in Arizona and California. Santa Fe rails had first reached into central Arizona after the Santa Fe, Prescott & Phoenix Railway was incorporated in 1891 to build from Ash Fork, on the Santa Fe (Atlantic & Pacific) main line to Phoenix. Once finished the line was to be leased to Santa Fe. Construction began in 1892 and followed rugged canyons south to Prescott and over the Sierra Prieta Mountains. South of Wickenburg the railroad passed through rugged, scenic Hassayampa Canyon, then across level desert country into Phoenix, which was reached in 1895. The railroad was nicknamed the "Peavine" a moniker the line still holds, because of the many twists and turns along the 197-mile route. Santa Fe purchased the Peavine outright in 1901 and, as per Santa Fe practice, carried out a series of improvements. In 1902, it

Late afternoon sun rays drench a westbound freight with warm light at Amarillo, Texas, in November 1970. With the opening of the Belen Cutoff, Amarillo became an important point on the railroad's new Chicago-California freight route. *Paul Enenbach*

Train 8, the *Fast Mail*, puts on a good show of steam and smoke as it accelerates out of La Junta, Colorado, during the late afternoon of March 31, 1929—on the eve of the Depression. *Railroad Museum of Pennsylvania*

built a new line to lessen curves and grades, including a high bridge over Hell Canyon at Drake, Arizona, which was 676 feet long and 170 feet high.

But passenger and freight trains destined from Phoenix to California still had to travel north to Ash Fork before reaching the main line. With the Phoenix area growing rapidly, President Ripley decided that a short cut to California was in order. Consequently the company chartered the Arizona & California Railway on September 10, 1903, to build from a connection with the Peavine at Wickenburg to the transcontinental main line at Cadiz, California, in the Mojave Desert. The first 100 miles of railroad, from Wickenburg to Parker, Arizona, on the Arizona-California border, was across desert country and was relatively easy to construct. This segment opened in 1907. However, at Parker the A&C had to build a bridge over the Colorado River to enter California, and this was not completed until 1908. A recession in 1907 also slowed construction, but the 87-mile gap from Parker to Cadiz was finally closed in 1910. Passenger and freight service began in July of that year, and Santa Fe carded a new Los Angeles-Phoenix passenger train, the *Phoenix Express*, operating on an overnight schedule. Later a section of the famous Los Angeles-Chicago *California Limited* served Phoenix, with cars added to

or taken off the *Limited* at Cadiz.

Eventually the Arizona & California name disappeared (though it would return in the 1990s; see Chapter 5) as it was absorbed by other Santa Fe subsidiaries, but a branch from its "main" line would play a part in yet another Santa Fe bypass project. As Southern California grew, the railroad considered building a shortcut route into San Diego which would bypass Cajon Pass and congestion in the Los Angeles area. The new line would connect with the old A&C at Rice and head southwest to a connection with an existing railroad near Plaster City, California, to gain entrance to San Diego.

To accomplish this task, the California Southern Railroad Company was incorporated in 1914. This was not the same California Southern which earlier had built Santa Fe lines in California; that railroad had been consolidated into another subsidiary railroad in 1889. The "new" CS constructed a 49-mile line from Rice to the town of Blythe, which was completed in 1916. Another seven miles south of Blythe was opened in 1921. Longtime Santa Fe president E. P. Ripley died in 1920 and in his honor, the end of track was named Ripley. Unfortunately, the railroad never made it beyond this point and Ripley became the end of an isolated branch line in an isolated corner of the vast Santa Fe system.

The Coleman Cutoff

Improvements weren't limited to the western part of the system. Santa Fe had a large presence in Texas and served most of its major cities, but freight headed west for California points first had to be routed north into Oklahoma or Kansas before it could head west. The opening of the Belen Cutoff offered the company another opportunity: it could build a new line to connect with the Belen Cutoff and shorten transit times for shipments out of Texas. Under the charter of the Pecos Valley & Northern Texas Railroad, construction began in 1907 on a new line from Canyon, just west of Amarillo, south over the High Plains through Plainview to Lubbock, Texas. This line opened in 1910 and would tie in with another new line being built from Lubbock 205 miles east to an existing line at Coleman to provide the new shortcut. Construction proceeded from both Lubbock and Coleman and linked up at Augustus, Texas. The "Coleman Cutoff" opened for business in December 1911. Ripley delayed building the shortcut west of Lubbock to a link with the Belen Cutoff hoping for financial aide from communities and landowners, but eventually went ahead with construction regardless. The additional 88 miles of line from Lubbock to a connection with the Belen Cutoff at Texico opened in 1914, and the Coleman Cutoff was complete. The additional Texas traffic helped the Belen Cutoff reach its full potential, and in the 1990s the line across New Mexico was one of busiest on the Santa Fe, serving as a "funnel" for traffic from Chicago, Kansas City, and Texas destined to California points, and vice versa.

Other Improvements

As Santa Fe and its and freight and passenger traffic grew during the early twentieth century, so did the size of its steam locomotives. The larger the locomotive, the more cars it could pull with a single crew in the cab. If smaller locomotives were used on long trains, this resulted in the use of more than one engine, increasing crew costs. Consequently, Santa Fe worked with locomotive manufacturers to increase the size and pulling power of its steam locomotives. In 1902 the railroad's mechanical department worked with the Baldwin Locomotive Works of Philadelphia to perfect a larger locomotive. In 1903 their joint effort produced a huge locomotive with two leading wheels, ten driving wheels, and, in a new design, two trailing wheels to support a large firebox which produced more power. Since it was a

Freight Extra 231 West (an "Extra" is a non-scheduled train) is in the Tecific siding near Sweetwater, Texas, in May 1968 to await an opposing train. Sweetwater was about the midway point on the Coleman Cutoff. *Tom Hoffmann*

In a scene dating from pre-World War I era, lanky 4-6-0 No. 518 rolls along with a freight train near Chicago, possibly along the Des Plaines River, which the AT&SF followed into the heart of the city. *Railroad Museum of Pennsylvania*

design never used before, it was named the "Santa Fe" type in honor of the railroad. Over the next ten years AT&SF received 192 of the Santa Fes with the 2-10-2 wheel arrangement, and in the period from 1919 to 1927 purchased 140 more. The first 2-10-2s were the harbingers of even larger steam-locomotive designs the company would receive during the 1930s and 1940s (see Chapter 7).

Another area where Santa Fe displayed its leadership was in the development of oil-burning locomotives. Since it first began running trains across the deserts of New Mexico, Arizona, and California, the company had been forced to transport coal into these areas to keep its locomotives fueled. In addition to the high cost of transportation, some coal burned poorly and caused cinders to fly down the right-of-way, creating a fire hazard. In 1905 Union Oil Company of California and Santa Fe jointly developed an oil-burning locomotive (Southern Pacific had been approached by Union Oil first, but turned the company down). At Santa Fe's large shop complex in San Bernardino, Union Oil and Santa Fe converted a small 4-4-0-type locomotive to successfully burn oil. Since oil fields were plentiful in the West, the company quickly converted most of its steam locomotives to oil burners, leaving only the Chicago-Kansas City route in the hands of coal-burning engines.

The "Scott Special"

Early on, Santa Fe established a reputation for speed. In 1889 New York reporter Nelly Bly traveled around the world in a challenge to Phileas Fogg, the fictional character in Jules Verne's book AROUND THE WORLD IN 80 DAYS. In 1890 she arrived in San Francisco and climbed aboard a Santa Fe special train to Chicago, which covered the distance in 69 hours at an average speed of 37 miles per hour. Ms. Bly arrived in New York in 72 days, beating Fogg's fictional record. In 1895 another special run made it from California to Chicago in 57 hours, and in 1903 another Los Angeles-Chicago record was set when a train ran the distance in just over 52 hours. But the trip of Walter Scott in 1905 from Los Angeles to Chicago was the most memorable of the high-speed trips and propelled Santa Fe into the national spotlight.

Scott, better known as "Death Valley Scotty," was a well-to-do cowboy with a reputation for being eccentric. At one time he had been a trick rider in Buffalo Bill's Wild West Show before making his fortune in mining in a canyon above Death Valley. On July 8, 1905, he walked into Santa Fe's Los Angeles offices and demanded a trip to Chicago in 46 hours, a time which had never been achieved before. Could the Santa Fe do it? Lines West General Passenger Agent John Byrne thought it could, and for the then-astronomical sum of

$5,500 an agreement was made. The train would depart Los Angeles the next day.

Dubbed the "Coyote Special," the three-car train departed L.A.'s La Grande Station the next afternoon. The railroad recognized the enormous publicity value of the run, and the publicity department worked to alert press across the country of Scotty's run. Being a weekend, a huge crowd came to the depot to watch the special depart at 1 p.m. July 9, 1905. The train roared out of Los Angeles and into San Bernardino, where a helper engine coupled on for the trip up Cajon Pass. At the summit of the pass the helper cut off without stopping—uncoupling "on the fly" and moving into a siding. Between the Summit and Barstow the train hit 96 mph. En route, Scotty and his party dined on specially-prepared gourmet foods as the train slammed around curves, at times throwing food to the floor.

Along the way, Santa Fe sent out track workers a half hour before the special's arrival to inspect track, bridges, and switches. After crossing Arizona and New Mexico it climbed Raton Pass, then headed onto the flat, fast track east of La Junta where speeds reached up to 90 mph. Along the way, dispatches were dropped off the train to agents who telegraphed its progress to an excited nation. Scotty even sent a wire to President Theodore Roosevelt. Across Kansas, Missouri, and Illinois Scotty's special roared on, reaching a top speed of 106 mph near Cameron (near Galesburg), Illinois. From Fort Madison to Chicago's Dearborn Station the special covered 239 miles in 239 minutes.

The train pulled into Dearborn at 11:54 a.m. on July 11, having made the trip from Los Angeles in 44 hours, 54 minutes, an average speed of 50.4 miles per hour. The new record made headlines across the country, garnering Santa Fe fame as a high-speed railroad and further enhancing Death Valley Scotty's reputation. Scott made a more sedate trip a few days later, traveling on the *California Limited* back to Los Angeles.

While Santa Fe pulled out all the stops to ensure the special would make record time, perhaps even more remarkable was the fact the railroad achieved this goal with only about 24 hours' notice. The company employed its regular locomotives and

crews, who simply stretched the limits of speed and equipment, testimony to the fact that even in its adolescence the AT&SF was a well-maintained railroad. The only special treatment shown on Scotty's record-shattering run was that his train was given superiority over all others on the railroad, including regular passenger runs, which cleared out of the way for the "Coyote Special." One locomotive from this famous trip, 2-6-2 No. 1010, which handled the train from Needles to Seligman, Arizona, has been preserved at the California State Railroad Museum in Sacramento.

World War I

Santa Fe was well recognized as a strong, prosperous railroad as the first World War broke out across Europe in 1914. Traffic, particularly foodstuffs and ammunition, flowed across the railroads to ships destined for worn-torn countries. With the entrance of the U.S. into World War I in 1917, traffic boomed, particularly along railroads in the Northeast. Traffic logjams and a threat of labor unrest spurred the federal government into action, and U.S. President Woodrow Wilson nationalized the U.S. railroads under the Federal Possession and Control Act on December 28, 1917. The United States Railroad Administration (USRA) was formed to operate and pay railroads for the use of their systems. Under the nationalization plan, the USRA paid the railroads equal to the average net operating income during the previous three years ending on June 30, 1917. At the end of the war, the USRA would return the railroads to their owners.

Generally the Santa Fe fared well under federal control, but several changes were made. Ticket offices of several railroads were combined, and off-line traffic offices were closed. Traffic was routed over the most efficient routes regardless of railroad, and the railroads repaired each others' equipment. The overall goal was to keep traffic moving regardless of which railroad line it was moving over. Losses rose and railroad leaders sought higher rates from the government, which was granted in 1918, but did not have much impact due to escalating costs—particularly labor costs and taxes.

AT&SF President Ripley had long been

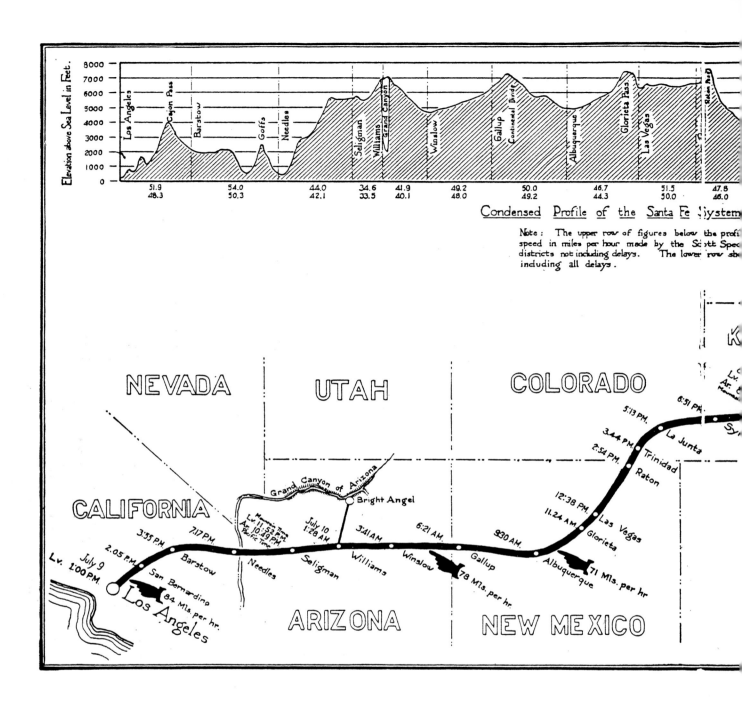

Condensed Profile of the Santa Fe System

Note: The upper row of figures below the profile [...] speed in miles per hour made by the Scott Spec[ial] districts not including delays. The lower row sh[ows] including all delays.

an opponent of organized labor. He had instituted several programs across the railroad in an attempt to keep workers satisfied and stave off union organization, including wage increases directly related to the quality of work, an apprentice program, creation of an employee magazine, and pension plans. Yet the power of labor grew and was greatly increased under nationalization. USRA greatly increased workers' wages. Working with the unions, blanket contracts were signed which applied to all railroads, including AT&SF. Despite Rip-

ley's hopes and actions, almost total unionization came to the Santa Fe. Workers did not wish to give up their gains after the war, and Santa Fe remained a "union shop." Employment reached its peak on the Santa Fe under government control, with 82,059 employees on the payroll.

The USRA managed to lose huge amounts of money, and President Wilson wanted to return the railroads to private ownership; he did so on March 1, 1920. The nationalization experiment, while not inflicting nearly as much financial and

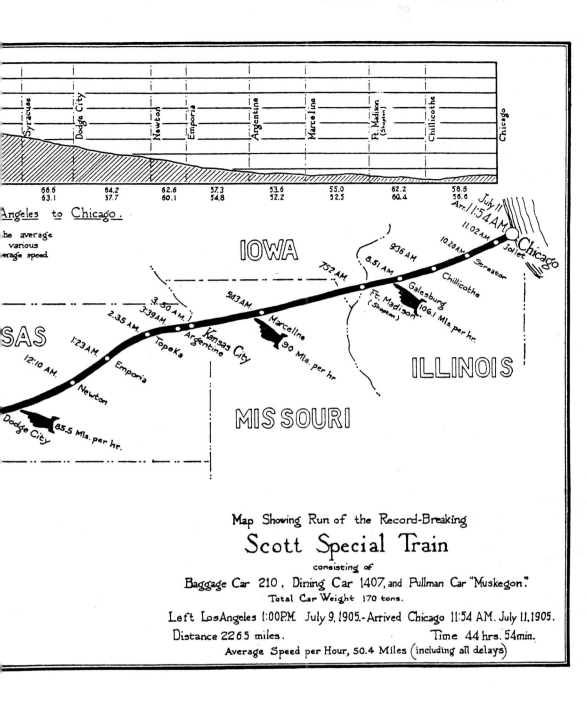

Map Showing Run of the Record-Breaking
Scott Special Train
consisting of
Baggage Car 210, Dining Car 1407, and Pullman Car "Muskegon."
Total Car Weight 170 tons.

Left LosAngeles 1:00 P.M. July 9, 1905.- Arrived Chicago 11:54 A.M. July 11, 1905.
Distance 2265 miles.   Time 44 hrs. 54 min.
Average Speed per Hour, 50.4 Miles (including all delays)

Even by modern-day standards, the Scott Special's trip over Santa Fe's "traditional" Chicago-California route (that by way of Raton Pass) was a notable accomplishment. Though it was a one-time event, it early on provided a foundation for Santa Fe's reputation as a high-speed Midwest-California operation. Even during the Amtrak era when that carrier fielded several passenger route options between Chicago and California, those train which followed the path plied by the Scott Special and later the *Chiefs* was always the fastest. *Railroad Museum of Pennsylvania.*

physical damage on AT&SF as it did on other roads, nonetheless could largely be considered a failure. The experiment would not be repeated when the U.S. again faced war 21 years later.

Post-World War I Improvements

During the "Roaring '20s" the population in Santa Fe's service area grew, as did the amount of freight it hauled. Under the leadership of President William Benson Storey, who succeeded Ripley, the company expanded the efforts of its industrial department. Santa Fe's agriculture and livestock departments had been responsible for much of the traffic growth prior to the 1920s, but with America gradually turning from an agrarian to industrial society, the contributions of the industrial department became more significant. It promoted the development of industry along Santa Fe lines, including developing a new produce terminal in Chicago, opening a new warehouse and office building in Dallas, and developing a massive industrial center in Los Angeles, which boomed in the

1920s and again during and following World War II.

Improvements to the physical plant continued. Locomotive shops were modernized: Albuquerque was updated in 1921-23, San Bernardino was modernized between 1924 and 1927, and the Cleburne, Texas, shop facility was upgraded between 1928 and 1930. Mirroring the program begun under Ripley, track improvements were made as well. In 1924 the railroad built a new 47-mile cutoff between Ellinor and El Dorado, Kansas. Traveling through the scenic Flint Hills area of the state, the new cutoff shortened the route for trains traveling to/from Texas points and the Belen Cutoff and essentially completed what is today's main transcontinental freight route between Chicago and Los Angeles. Three years later a new swing-span bridge was opened across the Mississippi River at Fort Madison, Iowa, replacing a structure built in 1887.

The yard and shop complex at San Bernardino, California—shown in this scene dating from the 1970s—benefitted from a major upgrading undertaken during the mid-1920s, which made the location among the most important on the whole Santa Fe system. *Jim Boyd*

The "Orient" and other additions

In 1929, Santa Fe acquired yet another railroad and merged it into its system. On October 19 the Kansas City, Mexico & Orient Railway (KCM&O), operating between Wichita, Kansas, and Alpine, Texas, was acquired. The "Orient," as it was nicknamed, was the dream of Arthur E. Stilwell, a Kansas City real-estate and insurance executive who also founded the Kansas City Southern Railway. His hope was to build a railroad that would link Kansas City and the Gulf of California at the port of Topolobampo, Mexico. Stilwell's railroad cut across Kansas, Oklahoma, and Texas and would have created a direct route from Kansas City to the Gulf of California 400 miles shorter than a line built directly to the Pacific Coast. Stilwell's hope was that the new, shorter route would promote trade with the Orient, hence the grandiose name of the railroad.

Construction began at Anthony, Kansas,

southwest of Wichita and was complete through Oklahoma and into Texas by 1909. By 1913 the railroad had reached Alpine. Construction work was also being conducted from Topolobampo east to the Sierra Madre mountains. But investors gradually withdrew from the project, and the Mexican segment fell pray to the revolution in that country. Alpine was as far as the "Orient" would get. Until the railroad was complete, it could not earn the revenues which had been projected, and a lack of revenue kept it from being completed. KCM&O entered receivership in 1912, but remained alive into the 1920s. Wanting to prevent another carrier from taking over the line and getting a foothold in its territory, the Santa Fe in 1928 acquired the company for $14 million. The new acquisition would also serve as a cutoff for some freight bound for Kansas City and Chicago from the Great Plains. Santa Fe wanted only the U.S. lines, and in 1929 sold off the 320 miles in Mexico. Eventually these lines were acquired by the Mexican government, which improved them and pushed for their completion, although that did not occur until 1961.

AT&SF extended the old Orient line from Alpine to the Mexican border at Presidio, and improved the connections it had with the former KCM&O line farther north, but as branch lines declined in importance so did the value of the Orient to the Santa Fe. Later several portions of the former KCM&O main line were pulled up. In 1991

the northern end of the railroad from Maryneal, Texas, to Cherokee, Oklahoma, was sold to the Texas & Oklahoma Railroad, and in 1992 the southern section from San Angelo, Texas, to Presidio was sold to shortline South Orient Railroad Co., Ltd. for $5.5 million.

Another railroad acquired by Santa Fe was the Clinton & Oklahoma Western, the "COW" line, operating between Clinton, Oklahoma, and Pampa, Texas. Picked up in 1928, this route became a source of wheat and livestock business, and eventually the Texas oil boom also contributed to revenues. It was abandoned in 1981.

The expansion of the Santa Fe system made it the largest railroad in the United States, a title it held for many years. Peak mileage was 13,568 miles, reached in 1931. But while the system grew larger during the 1920s, Santa Fe's passenger business began to decline. Highways were improving and more Americans turned to the private automobile for transportation. The stockmarket crash in 1929 and the Depression which followed in the 1930s made matters even worse. But Santa Fe was not about to let the automobile take all its passenger business without a fight. Beginning in the mid-1930s, the railroad would take several steps which would earn the company an unparalleled reputation for fine service and bring many travelers back to the rails. That, and Santa Fe's progress in the face of Depression and another war, are the subjects of following chapters.

Freights pass on the Santa Fe main line at Ellinor, Kansas, in June 1985. Ellinor, 13 miles west of Emporia, Kansas, was and is the starting point of the Ellinor Cutoff, which in part provides through freights a shortcut to Wellington, Kansas, bypassing the congestion of Wichita if necessary. *Scott Muskopf*

Orient bought 7/1928
COW

Out of the depths of the Depression came a silver lining for Santa Fe—a fleet of new, stainless-steel streamliners that would put the railroad at a world-class level in terms of passenger services. The post-Depression years also marked the birth of what would be one of the railroad's most-enduring slogans, "Santa Fe All The Way," which the railroad's sidekick, Chico, is writing in the sand of this memorable Santa Fe ad. Meanwhile, in the distance, new Electro-Motive E1s speed their way across the Southwest with the new streamlined *Super Chief*.
Joe Welsh Collection

Depression, War, and Beyond

1930-1959

3

As Santa Fe worked through the Depression and into the World War II years, leadership of the company changed, but it remained a strong, viable entity. While many railroads fell into bankruptcy during the Depression, the Santa Fe was not among them, despite dramatic decreases in traffic and revenues.

Surviving the Depression

President William B. Storey retired in 1933 and was replaced by Samuel T. Bledsoe. Bledsoe differed from his predecessors in that he did not come from the operating or engineering departments, but was an attorney by trade. He had previously served as the company's general counsel before being elevated into management ranks. Upon him fell the task of leading Santa Fe through the Depression and the "Dust Bowl."

Beginning in 1930, thousands of miles of fertile farm and cattle land suffered under a tremendous drought. Lack of crop rotation, overuse of the land and the drought combined to create the Dust Bowl, with valuable topsoil virtually stripped away by the wind. Unfortunately, Santa Fe's service area included much of the Dust Bowl in Oklahoma and Texas, and the loss of agriculture and livestock traffic produced the worst traffic losses in the railroad's history.

Cutting costs was one way to ease the strain on the railroad. With the decline in revenues, shop and maintenance crews were laid off and many programs were put on hold. Dividends were lowered and for a time discontinued and wages were cut. Under Bledsoe's tenure, more than 300 miles of marginal branch lines were abandoned. But Bledsoe also instituted track improvement programs in the 1930s, such as elevating curves on the Chicago-Los Angeles main line to allow higher speeds. Hundreds of miles of new, heavier rail was laid.

The year 1936 marked the beginning of a new era for Santa Fe when, on May 12, it inaugurated the *Super Chief* in response to competing new passenger services being introduced by rival Union Pacific. Though this first rendition of the *Super Chief* was not streamlined, it was diesel-powered and represented Santa Fe's first application of diesel power for over-the-road train service.

A year later, Santa Fe entered the streamliner era with the inauguration of the streamlined *Super Chief* in 1937. In addition to passenger service, freight service was improved with a speed-up in freight schedules and the purchase of over 3,000 freight cars and new freight diesels to pull them. Full-page ads were run in several national publications to encourage more business. For many years Santa Fe used the slogan "Santa Fe All The Way" in bold italics on its freight equipment, delivering to all the message that it was the only railroad with single-line service from Chicago all the way to California.

Even in the throes of the Depression, improvements in routes continued with the construction of yet another "cutoff." The Santa Fe had long played second fiddle to the Burlington in moving traffic between Texas and Colorado. Through subsidiaries Colorado & Southern and Fort Worth & Denver, Burlington had by far the shortest route between the Gulf of Mexico and Colorado. In the 1920s as agriculture expand-

In the thick of the Depression, commerce still moves on the Santa Fe as 4-8-2 3879 slugs over Cajon Pass with 46 cars of westbound tonnage. Date: April 26, 1933. *Railroad Museum of Pennsylvania*

ed and oil discoveries increased the potential for rail traffic in the area, Santa Fe acted. The company made an application with the Interstate Commerce Commission (ICC) to construct 220 miles of new railroad from Amarillo, Texas, through Boise City, Oklahoma, to Las Animas, Colorado, where it would connect with the northern transcontinental main line just east of La Junta. The ICC gave its blessing in 1930. Crews built 121 miles of new track from Amarillo to Boise City in 1931, but were stopped by the decline in revenues caused by the Depression and the Dust Bowl. Construction resumed in 1936 and 111 miles of track from Boise City to Las Animas was laid. The new line was opened on February 1, 1937, with the governor of Colorado pounding home a "golden spike" at a special ceremony. The new line cost $3.75 million.

Santa Fe also shortened its route from Fort Worth to California when it purchased 215 miles of branchline track from the Frisco. The trackage, which was in poor condition, ran from Fort Worth to Menard,

Texas, and crossed the Coleman Cutoff at Brownwood. The AT&SF plan was to rehabilitate the branch between Fort Worth and Brownwood to serve as a cutoff for Fort Worth-California traffic: it would shorten the route by 117 miles. Santa Fe paid financially-strapped Frisco over a million dollars for the line, which it purchased March 2, 1937. In use as a main line for 55 years, Santa Fe dropped the line as a through route in September 1992, when it switched to trackage rights over 196 miles of Union Pacific ex-Texas & Pacific track from Fort Worth to Sweetwater, Texas, which further shortened its Texas-California route.

It was during this same period—the late 1930s—that Santa Fe was investing heavily in streamlined passenger cars and inaugurating new trains: in the 14-month period from May 1937 to July 1938 the company streamlined the *Chief* and *Super Chief*, while *El Capitan*, the *Golden Gate*, and the *San Diegan* streamliners entered service. The year 1937 turned out to be the best for traffic since 1931.

CHAPTER 3

Bledsoe fell ill and died in 1939. He was succeeded by Edward J. Engel, who served until 1944. He also rose through the management ranks, rather than the operating department. He continued the improvements planned by Bledsoe and guided the company into the enormous traffic growth caused by World War II.

The World War II Era

Traffic began a rebound in 1939, and the company put more money into capital expenditures, with $25 million budgeted. Chicago's Dearborn Station (owned by the Chicago & Western Indiana, a subsidiary Santa Fe jointly owned with other Chicago-based railroads) was remodeled, and a new station and office building opened in Galveston, Texas. The major improvement that year was the opening of the new Los Angeles Union Passenger Terminal (LAUPT). The new station replaced Santa Fe's elegant but aging La Grande Station, which had opened in 1893. The new terminal had 16 tracks and covered 48 acres, with a square clock tower which rose 125 feet above the Spanish-style depot building. The station was connected with eight loading platforms by nearly 500 feet of subway thoroughfares. LAUPT was paid for by its three main tenants: Santa Fe, Southern Pacific, and Union Pacific. Southern Pacific owned 44%, Union Pacific 33%, and Santa Fe

23% of the terminal. Special opening ceremonies for the new station where held on Wednesday, May 3, 1939, with a grand parade down Alameda Street that drew more than 500,000 onlookers. All three railroads brought out their best, newest equipment for the event and movie stars could be found in abundance. LAUPT opened for regular service on Sunday, May 7, 1939. The first Santa Fe "name" train to enter the terminal that day was the *Scout*, pulled by 4-8-4 No. 3751. La Grande continued to serve as extra office space until it was torn down in 1946.

The onset of World War II meant huge increases in traffic for U.S. railroads, Santa Fe among them. Railroads moved an average of 5,000 cars of war goods each day to various military sites across the nation. Passenger traffic boomed during the war as troops headed west for the fighting in the Pacific Theater. For example, before the war LAUPT was handling 33 trains in and out from three railroads. During the conflict it was handling more than 100 trains daily. U.S. railroads transported 1.5 million armed services personnel every six months which required the operation of 3,000 special trains. Santa Fe passenger traffic rose 88% between 1941 and 1942, and the amount of freight moved nearly doubled. Manpower shortages were acute, and women were employed in nearly all crafts

At one time a branch out of Lamy, New Mexico, ran south through to Willard, New Mexico, on the Belen Cutoff offering a short cut between the original main and the Cutoff. On April 17, 1933, mixed train No. 77 prepares to depart Lamy for its 135-mile round trip to Willard. *Railroad Museum of Pennsylvania*

Santa Fe's new Electro-Motive road passenger diesels 1A and 1B— alias "Amos 'n' Andy"— greet crowds at Pasadena station on May 21, 1936, with the second westbound run of the *Super Chief*. The new train was Santa Fe's answer to rival Union Pacific's new streamliner *City of Los Angeles*, which had been inaugurated on May 15. Although the new *Super Chief* was an all-heavyweight (non streamlined) train for its first year of existence, it matched the running time of the *City of Los Angeles* and provided unequaled service. Santa Fe initially was concerned that the *Super Chief* would siphon passengers from what had been the carrier's premier train, the *Chief*, but the opposite happened: the *Super* enticed people in general to return to the rails and ridership went up on all principal Santa Fe trains. *Railroad Museum of Pennsylvania*

DEPRESSION, WAR, AND BEYOND   43

On May 18, 1937, the first streamlined *Super Chief* (shown posing for publicity photos near Chicago) entered service. Electro-Motive supplied new E1-type passenger diesels for the *Super* while the Edward G. Budd Manufacturing Company built the rolling stock. Initially, there was only a single set of *Super Chief* equipment, thus the *Super* made but a single Chicago-L.A. round trip per week. Interestingly, a traction-motor problem preventing the new E1s from debuting on the first streamlined *Super* which instead ran behind "Amos" and an Electro-Motive box-cab demonstrator locomotive. *Santa Fe Railway*

for the first time. Employment rose dramatically and eventually over 58,000 were employed.

Not only military traffic increased. With Europe under siege, the U.S. production of foodstuffs increased. Santa Fe had always been a leading grain carrier and became even more so during the war. However, the railroads did not profit from wartime traffic as much as might be expected. Railroads which had received land grants from the government had to abide by a 50% discount for all military traffic. Consequently many railroads suffered significant losses in potential revenue, including Santa Fe. Another restriction was an increase in the corporate income tax and a new excess profits tax during the war.

In 1944 Engel retired and was replaced by Fred G. Gurley, who served as president until 1957. Gurley was an operating man who loved diesels and new technology. His presidency would be one of the most progressive of any Santa Fe leader as the road completed dieselization, revitalized physical plant, and added even more streamliners.

Santa Fe was an early proponent of centralized traffic control (CTC), which allows dispatchers to line up tracks and signals from hundreds of miles away without the need for written train orders which can bog down train movement. For example, if done with the proper timing, CTC allows one train to enter a siding to meet another train without either train stopping (assuming the siding was long enough). An early CTC installation, in conjunction with SP, was over the Tehachapi Mountains of California. By the time of the merger with BN, CTC had been extended over nearly the entire Chicago-California transcontinental line and the main line into Texas. In many areas Santa Fe had installed CTC over track segments which were double track, allowing trains to move in either direction on either track. This flexibility allowed dispatchers to move higher priority trains around slower ones without either train having to stop.

The Santa Fe also employed radio communications at an early date (1944), allowing engine-to-caboose communication.

Radio communication was quickly expanded across the system. The Gurley administration also pushed for line improvements, including heavier rail, double-tracking, and terminal improvements.

Santa Fe Skyway

One of the more interesting aspects Santa Fe history was Santa Fe Skyway, Inc. In 1946 Gurley announced the formation of this operation, which would provide contract air freight transportation in areas served by the railroad. The company obtained two surplus Douglas C-47s (the military version of the DC-3 aircraft), which were adorned with the famous Santa Fe cross logo just behind the cockpit. The "Goony Birds," as DC-3s were affectionately called by pilots, could handle 5,500 pounds of cargo at speeds up to 190 mph. Headquarters for the new air freight operation was at Wichita, and it was to fly between the Midwest, California, and Texas. Service began July 31, 1946, with a flight from Salinas, California, to Chicago for the Fred Harvey Company.

In September 1946 Santa Fe Skyway applied to the Civil Aeronautics Board (CAB) for permission to operate as a common carrier over three routes: Los Angeles and San Francisco to Chicago and Chicago to Dallas/Fort Worth. In 1947 while awaiting the CAB decision, four more aircraft joined the fleet, which was used to transport perishable items such as flowers and fruit. By the time of its first birthday it was one of the top charter freight carriers operating into Los Angeles. But in December

Santa Fe went all out once it got into the dieselization process. The railroad was an early proponent of Electro-Motive's popular F-series road freight locomotive and bought EMC's first model of that series—the FT—in large quantities. In this scene on Cajon Pass in 1941, two FT pairs make their first revenue trip over the Santa Fe. *Railroad Museum of Pennsylvania*

1947 the CAB denied Santa Fe Skyway permission to operate as a common carrier. The Board claimed that airlines were not engaged in trucking or building railroads, and that operating the air freight service in conjunction with railroad operations was not a "coordinated" service and therefore would not be permitted. Gurley appealed the decision to another Commission, but was denied for the same reason and the Skyway was out of business.

This was not the first time that the Santa Fe Railway had participated in air transport. Back in 1928 it was a participant in Transcontinental Air Transport, Inc. (TAT), which sought to carry passengers between New York and Los Angeles using a combination of airplanes and trains. Passengers would use the Pennsylvania Railroad out of New York, departing at night since planes at that time could be used only during daylight hours. After getting a good night's sleep in a Pullman, passengers awoke in Columbus, Ohio, where

Even passenger trains required assistance to surmount Raton Pass. In this 1942 scene, a 2-10-2 helps hoist the all-coach streamliner *El Capitan* over the 3.5% grades of Raton. *R. H. Kindig, Railroad Museum of Pennsylvania*

they boarded a TAT flight for Waynoka, Oklahoma (with intermediate stops at Indianapolis, St. Louis, and Kansas City) where they boarded a Santa Fe train at dusk. The Santa Fe transported the passengers to Clovis where they boarded a TAT flight for Los Angeles. The service began on July 7, 1929, with Col. Charles A. Lindberg at the controls of the first flight between Columbus and Waynoka. But the service just got going when the stockmarket crash occurred and quickly ended.

The Baby Boom Era

In the postwar era more expansion was in the offing. Gurley had plans for a major expansion, this time to extend Santa Fe's reach into St. Louis—a goal for the company since the days of William Barstow Strong. The plan would have required no new construction, as it involved the Chicago, Burlington & Quincy, which was planning to improve its Kansas City-St. Louis route. Gurley and Burlington President Ralph Budd came up with a plan under

Alco PA passenger diesels on eastbound train 60, the Richmond-Bakersfield (California) *Golden Gate*, overtake a Cab-Forward powering an SP freight in the Tehachapis on October 14, 1950. At the time, the *Golden Gate* handled through cars for the Bakersfield section of the *Grand Canyon*. *William D. Middleton*

which they would jointly purchase 156 miles of track from the Gulf, Mobile & Ohio from Kansas City to Mexico, Missouri (over which CB&Q had trackage rights), and rehabilitate it; the GM&O would receive trackage rights over the rebuilt line to continue its service. From Mexico, trains would use Burlington tracks into St. Louis. Santa Fe also agreed to grant Burlington rights over parts of the Chicago-Kansas City "airline" in Missouri to help the latter road improve its own route between the two cities. All three roads ratified the agreement.

Once again, though, regulators derailed Santa Fe's plans. Opposition to the St. Louis route expansion was drummed up by competitors Frisco, Missouri Pacific, Rock Island, and St. Louis-Southwestern (Cotton Belt), which feared a Santa Fe invasion of their territory. An ICC examiner ruled negatively on the plan, and in 1948 the Commission denied the railroad's request on the basis that it would negatively effect the other railroads, some of which were in weak financial position. It would be the 1990s before Santa Fe would finally achieve its goal of reaching St. Louis.

The postwar era was a golden one for passenger services. The famed *Super Chief* and *El Capitan* became daily trains in 1948 as enough new streamlined equipment arrived to expand them. The same year a new service between Chicago and Galveston began, the *Texas Chief*. In 1951 the *Super Chief* received more new equipment, as did several other streamliners (see Chapter 6).

Through the early 1950s the company prospered, even as the first hints of financial problems began to be seen on other roads, particularly in the East. Ever seeking to better its route structure, AT&SF took steps in the mid-1950s to improve its service to Dallas. At the time, Santa Fe served Dallas via a dead-end spur, which extended north from Cleburne, Texas (on the Chicago-Houston-Galveston route), through Dallas to Paris, Texas. There was no direct access to Dallas from the north. Freight had to follow the roundabout route through Cleburne, and passengers to and from the north were bused between Fort Worth and Dallas. To resolve the situation, a new line was constructed from Dalton Junction, just south of Sanger, Texas, to Zacha Junction, near Garland on the Cleburne-Paris branch. Construction on the $7 million, 46-mile line began in 1954 and the new route opened on December 1,

1955, thus enabling Dallas traffic to be routed north or south depending on points of origin or destination. The railroad also inaugurated a Dallas section of the *Texas Chief* to directly serve "Big D" which was split (southbound) or combined (northbound) with the main section at Gainesville, Texas. This route remained intact until parts of it were sold to Dallas Area Rapid Transit and Kansas City Southern between 1992 and 1995, and Santa Fe exited Dallas completely.

Another new line was built in California. A 29.5-mile branch line opened from Hesperia (near Cajon Pass) to Cushenbury in 1956. The line was built to serve a Kaiser Permanente Cement Company mine.

Freight service was expanded and trains speeded up in the 1950s and 1960s. The advertising department, in addition to promoting the expansive passenger service along Santa Fe lines, began taking out ads touting freight service aimed at potential shippers. Studies showed that several commodities such as livestock, certain petroleum products, and "less than carload" (LCL) business was declining, while manufactured goods, coal, and potash were on the

Santa Fe steam in twilight: Engine 4051, a 2-8-2, appears to be making good time on a southbound Extra with 72 cars of mixed freight at Soldani, Oklahoma, on the Newkirk-Shawnee-Pauls Valley line in the central part of the state. *Railroad Museum of Pennsylvania*

Screaming through the desert north of Albuquerque in 1954, *El Capitan* shows off its new Big Dome lounge car at the center of the train. Domes were just one of several postwar improvements in Santa Fe passenger service. *David W. Salter*

increase. Service was increased to daily on lines which previously had less than everyday service while mainline trains were speeded up. New branch lines were built in New Mexico to reach potash mines. Santa Fe made a concerted effort to pursue produce traffic from California, with long strings of refrigerated cars—"reefers"—making their way east. Santa Fe invested in new cars for this service. The company benefited greatly from its location in America's Southwest, which saw explosive growth and prosperity in the quarter century following the end of World War II. As the Southwest grew, so did the Santa Fe.

In 1957 Gurley retired as president, moving up to chairman of Santa Fe's board and chief executive officer. He was replaced in the presidency by Ernest K. Marsh, who had been employed by the Santa Fe since 1918. Marsh had moved up through the executive ranks to achieve the presidency and replaced Gurley as CEO in 1958. Despite the cost savings achieved with dieselization, which was completed in 1957, Marsh faced increasing costs as taxes were increased, losses from passenger train operations mounted, and labor costs rose. To Marsh's and Santa Fe's credit, they recognized that

while cutting costs was necessary to decrease expenses, increasing revenues was also important. Increasing revenue meant meeting its competition head on, and Santa Fe recognized early on that competition came mainly from trucks, not from other railroads. From 1958 through 1964, railroad freight revenues remained static, while those of truckers rose 49 percent. Even when rail rates dropped and trucking rates increased, motor carriers still picked up even more business. Railroads needed to battle back not only with rates, but with service as well.

To meet the challenge motor carriers presented, Santa Fe would have to once again speed up schedules and provide better service. This translated into spending more on track improvements and purchasing modern locomotive and car fleets. AT&SF also wasn't bashful about putting truck trailers on its trains. In the 1960s and beyond, trailers on flatcars would be a common sight along the Santa Fe, until their numbers overtook traditional "boxcar" traffic which had been a staple of the railroad since its beginnings. These changes in the transportation industry dictated a major transition for the railroad, which is the subject of the following chapter.

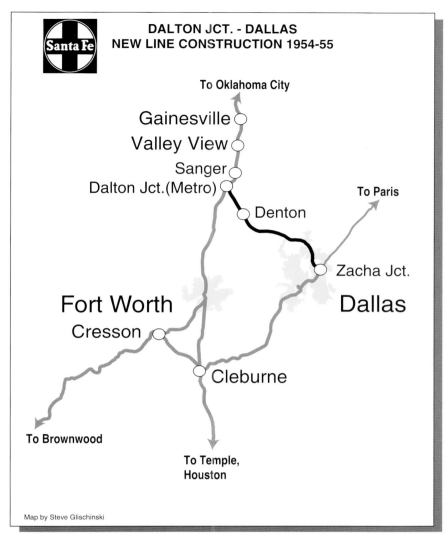

**DALTON JCT. - DALLAS
NEW LINE CONSTRUCTION 1954-55**

To Oklahoma City

Gainesville

Valley View

Sanger

Dalton Jct.(Metro)

Denton

To Paris

Zacha Jct.

Fort Worth

Dallas

Cresson

Cleburne

To Brownwood

To Temple,
Houston

Map by Steve Glischinski

Once Santa Fe opened its new route from the north into Dallas, the carrier wasted no time in establishing a Dallas section of the *Texas Chief*, which split from the main stem of train 15 (which passed through Fort Worth) at Gainesville, Texas. We're at the Gainesville station on July 15, 1967; No. 15 has already left for Fort Worth and Houston as the Dallas stub train, No. 115, prepares to head for Denton and "Big D" with the through Chicago-Dallas coach and sleeper. *Tom Hoffmann*

This scene on Edelstein Hill in Central Illinois imparts the look and feel of Santa Fe during the 1960s, when *Chief*s and other flyers still plied most of the railroad's main routes and newer freight locomotives were beginning to infiltrate the ranks of first-generation diesels. It's November 10, 1963, and the combined *Super Chief* and Hi-Level *El Capitan*, bound for Chicago, is beginning its descent into the Illinois River valley as a trio of GP20s hoists a westbound freight upgrade. The Prairie State may be synonymous with flat farmlands, but during the steam era, Edelstein Hill often required helpers. *Jim Boyd*

The Transition Years

1960–1990

4

The three decades between 1960 and 1990 were years of transition for the Santa Fe Railway. Not that the railroad hadn't seen considerable change during previous decades, but during the 1960-1990 period, the complexion of the railroad would almost completely change. Gone would be the *Chiefs* and other members of the passenger train "tribe," replaced by a tide of intermodal trains which would race at *Super Chief* speeds. Boxcar-laden freights trains would be relegated to minority status as the transition to intermodal was made. The diesel locomotives which replaced steam power would themselves be replaced with a second, and then a third generation of diesel power, the latter equipped with on-board computers. The government would finally lift much of the regulatory burden under which Santa Fe and other railroads had chafed since the 1880s. Finally, Santa Fe would attempt a merger with Southern Pacific that turned into an expensive venture leading to layoffs, downsizing, and other cost-saving measures as the company rebounded to a pre-eminent position among U.S. railroads.

Modernization and Expansion in the 1960s

In the 1960s the railroad expanded its capital budget to modernize the property. In 1960 the budget was $100 million, which was used to purchase new freight cars and diesels, welded rail (rail sections welded together in mile-long sections rather than being bolted together in 39-foot sections), and expanding the communications network. An even larger budget came in 1965 with a budget of $115 million which included orders for more than 4,000 freight cars.

One of the larger modernization projects involved the main line through northern Arizona. At this point, the railroad's traffic to and from California, Texas, and both the northern main lines has been funneled onto one line. The weak link in this busy artery was the 42-mile portion from Williams to Seligman via Ash Fork. At 5,250 feet, Ash Fork is 1,630 feet lower in elevation than Williams, 19 miles east. But 23 rail miles west at Seligman, the elevation is 100 feet higher. In between, at Crookton, the elevation gets up to 5,700 feet. Eastbound trains faced a rugged climb from Ash Fork to Williams along Ash Fork Draw, fighting 10-degree horseshoe curves and grades that required helpers.

To resolve the situation, Santa Fe began construction of an entirely new line from Williams to Crookton, known as the "Williams-Crookton Line Change" or sometimes just as the "Crookton Line Change." At 44-miles the new line was the largest new railroad construction project until Burlington Northern built a new line into the Wyoming coal fields during the 1970s. Santa Fe's new line was beautifully engineered, with the right-of-way blasted through deep cuts and across large fills to keep grades to a constant 1% from Crookton to Williams and allowing for high-speed operations which had been inhibited by the "up and down" profile of the old line. The new line was equipped with double-track and CTC-signaling, which allowed faster trains to run around slower trains at speed. The new line change cost $19.3 million and opened for business on December 19, 1960. The old line from Williams to Ash Fork was retained to provide a connection to the line to Phoenix; between Ash Fork and Crookton the old line was pulled up.

The Phoenix line itself was the subject

Three Electro-Motive GP20s ease into Joliet with an eastbound freight laden with perishables on a summer morning in 1966. These 2,000-hp diesels represented just one facet of a modernization plan which Santa Fe instituted in 1960. The new "turbocharged" diesels arrived on the property in 1960-61, replacing FT-type diesels the railroad had purchased some 20 years earlier. The GP20s were the most common type of road-freight power used between Kansas City and Chicago during the 1960s because they were equipped with cab signals necessary for the Chicago-K.C. route. *Mike Schafer*

of another major line change. The line between Ash Fork and Phoenix—nicknamed the "Peavine" for its twisting, curvy nature (see Chapter 2)—was the subject of a $3.5 million rebuilding completed in April 1962. A new, 37-mile line was constructed from Abra (29 miles south of Ash Fork), to Skull Valley, Arizona. The new route completely bypassed Prescott, Arizona, which ended up as part of a branch formed from the old line and permitted the abandonment of 23 miles of track over the Sierra Prieta Mountains (the remaining line into Prescott was abandoned in 1984 after tracks were washed out the year before). The total length of the Peavine was reduced by about 14 miles, and the new line had lesser grades. Helper locomotives were also eliminated, and only one train crew was needed to run trains between Ash Fork and Phoenix; previously crews had changed at Prescott. Santa Fe estimated that with all the changes, the new line would save the company $488,000 per year in operating costs.

Another acquisition in the 1960s was the Oklahoma City-Ada-Atoka Railway,

which Santa Fe purchased for $1 million in 1962. Operating 104 miles of track between Oklahoma City and Tupelo, Oklahoma, the line enabled Santa Fe to rationalize its Oklahoma branchline structure and provide access for freight traffic destined for Tinker Air Force Base.

In 1966 new mileage was added to the Santa Fe system with the construction of a 37.5-mile branch in northern New Mexico to serve Kaiser Steel's York Canyon coal mine. Coal from the mine would be used to power a Kaiser plant at Fontana, California. Santa Fe spent $4 million to build the branch from the main line at French, New Mexico, 31 miles south of Raton, to the mine. The first 18 miles of track were built on the grade of the former Dawson Railroad, which later became part of a SP branch that had been abandoned in 1952. Santa Fe purchased 101 new coal hoppers which were used in 84-car unit trains of coal, which shuttled between the mine and the California plant on a four-day cycle covering 2,164-miles round trip. The new line opened on September 28, 1966. The Fontana Mill closed in 1983, and the service ended, but in 1992 new service began.

CHAPTER 4

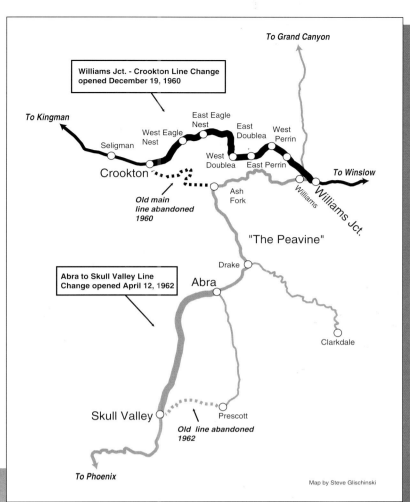

Williams Jct. - Crookton Line Change
opened December 19, 1960

To Kingman

Seligman

West Eagle
Nest

East Eagle
Nest

East
Doublea

West
Perrin

Crookton

West
Doublea

East Perrin

East
Perrin

Williams

To Winslow

Williams Jct.

To Grand Canyon

*Old main
line abandoned
1960*

Ash
Fork

"The Peavine"

Drake

Abra to Skull Valley Line
Change opened April 12, 1962

Abra

Clarkdale

Skull Valley

Prescott

*Old line abandoned
1962*

To Phoenix

Map by Steve Glischinski

BELOW: This 1990s view of a Houston-Bakersfield freight at Doublea, Arizona, illustrates a very important physical plant upgrade of the 1960s—that of the Crookton Line Change in northern Arizona. Numerous new cuts such as this as well as a radical line relocation between Williams Junction and Crookton vastly improved train operations on the Chicago-California main line. *Steve Glischinski.*

At the start of the 1960s, the vast majority of perishable traffic on the Santa Fe still moved in refrigerator cars. Special moves of such traffic were known as "Green Fruit Expresses" and often utilized spare passenger motive power or the use of the dual-service F-units such as illustrated by this westbound on its way out of Chicago in June 1966. *Jim Boyd*

Unit coal-train operations began that September between the mine, owned by Pittsburg & Midway Coal Mining, and a Wisconsin Electric power plant at Oak Creek, Wisconsin, near Milwaukee. Santa Fe moved the coal trains to McCook, Illinois, where they were turned over to the Chicago & North Western.

John S. Reed assumed the presidency of Santa Fe in January 1967 when Ernest S. Marsh moved up to chairman. Reed was a Yale graduate who came to Santa Fe in 1939, and worked in operations until 1954 when he moved into the executive area. (Reed was also a steam locomotive fan, and in 1976 seriously considered reactivating 4-8-4 No. 2925 for excursion service.)

In Reed's first year as president, he reluctantly had to announce the termination of many Santa Fe passenger trains after the U. S. Postal Service cancelled its contracts with Santa Fe and most other railroads that operated intercity passenger trains, which had provided much-needed revenue for the trains. To his credit, the passenger trains which remained after the cuts were operated with all the tradition and class the Santa Fe had been famous for right up until Amtrak took over most U.S. intercity passenger services in 1971.

The loss of some of Santa Fe's passenger trains in 1968 was offset that same year by the road's first in-depth experimentation into intermodal service—a story treated separately later in this chapter. Intermodal was destined to change the face of U.S. railroading in general and the Santa Fe in particular.

Santa Fe had long held interests in a variety of industries outside railroading, including lumber, oil, minerals, pipelines, real estate, and trucking among others. These other industries generally were doing well, while during the 1960s and 1970s many railroads were in precarious financial positions. While Santa Fe was on firm financial footing, it followed in the footsteps of many railroads by forming a holding company of which the railroad would be only one part. The holding company would be able to escape the regulatory restrictions placed on the railroad, had possible tax advantages, and permitted entry into what was seen as more profitable industries. In November 1967 the Santa Fe board authorized the formation of a new holding company, Santa Fe Industries (SFI). In 1968 railroad stockholders exchanged their holdings on a one-for-one basis for stock in SFI.

CHAPTER 4

Santa Fe of the 1970s

Reed successfully expanded SFI while continuing to invest in the railroad and pushing for cost reductions. In 1970 the board authorized a plan to abandon 815 miles of branch lines, but the proceedings before the ICC took the better part of the decade. In 1971 the railroad was relieved of its money-losing passenger service when it joined Amtrak—albeit at a cost of over $64 million. In the early 1970s the railroad

ABOVE: Although second-generation diesels arrived in droves during the 1960s, Electro-Motive F-units still held down numerous freight assignments. This set of blue-and-yellow Fs are in charge of a freight on the Coleman Cutoff at View, Texas, near Sweetwater, in 1967. *Tom Hoffmann.*

BELOW: The *Texas Chief*, hustling through Saginaw, Texas, in June 1969, was a survivor of the 1968 massacre that ended the likes of the *Chief, Chicagoan/Kansas Cityan,* and a host of secondary passenger runs like the Houston-Clovis *California Special*. *Tom Hoffmann.*

ABOVE: By the end of the 1960s, Santa Fe's diesel fleet had undergone a remarkable change, and the manner in which freight was hauled was beginning to be transformed as well. New F45 diesels sandwich older SD24s on this perishable train on which piggyback cars are beginning to replace reefers. *Dan Pope Collection*

RIGHT: Santa Fe joined Amtrak in 1971 and was thus relieved of the financial burden of passenger operation. Still looking like a Santa Fe train, Amtrak's *Super Chief/ El Capitan* cruises out of Chicago Union Station on a June evening in 1973. *Mike Schafer*

earned record revenue, and it continued to be the largest source of income for SFI.

A major rebuilding effort took place at Cajon Pass in California in 1972. At the top of the Pass at Summit station, a ten-degree curve severely limited operations and train speed. Santa Fe reworked the line, eliminating the curve and lowering the line 50 feet below the old alignment. The new trackage opened in September 1972, with an official "ribbon cutting" ceremony held on October 2. At the same time as the Summit curve was reworked, CTC was installed over the entire route from Barstow to San Bernardino. The new signal system was "reverse signaled" so trains could move in either direction on both tracks.

In 1975, in recognition

of the nation's Bicentennial, Santa Fe followed the suggestion of employee Joe McMillan in repainting locomotives in patriotic red, white, and blue colors. But unlike most lines, which painted a single locomotive, Santa Fe painted five Electro-Motive SD45-2s in Bicentennial dress. The locomotives regularly worked the *Super C* (more about this train in the next section) and other trains on the system, and were displayed at dozens of special events. Three of the locomotives assisted the *American Freedom Train* in early 1976 when it toured parts of the Santa Fe. The last of the five was repainted to the standard blue and yellow colors in 1978.

In the late 1970s Reed moved up to chairman of Santa Fe Industries and operating vice president Larry Cena moved into the president's chair. Cena was a proponent of intermodal and was key to expanding Santa Fe's intermodal business, which is a topic unto itself that transcends the 1950s into the 1990s.

Santa Fe Enters the Intermodal Age

Santa Fe's continuing commitment to improve and upgrade its route structure helped the railroad maintain its reputation for fast service. This reputation began during the passenger train era with trains such as Death Valley Scotty's record-setting "Coyote Special" and the luxurious *Super Chief*. But in the 1960s the age of privately operated passenger trains was winding down. Santa Fe's passenger fleet was shrinking, culminating in the massive petition to end most passenger service in 1967. But Santa Fe's wonderfully maintained, high-speed transcontinental main line remained, and as most of the passenger trains vanished, they were replaced by trailer-on-flatcar (TOFC) trains, also known as "piggyback" or "intermodal" trains.

Santa Fe first experimented with TOFC service in 1952 when several runs were made carrying dry ice containers containing semiperishable products. By 1954 Santa Fe offered piggyback service between Chicago and California and to the Gulf, but these were trailers handled in regular freight trains. Trucks, with ever better roads and the evolution of the federally funded Interstate highway system, began to cut into railroads' merchandise business by offering cheaper, faster, and more reli-

able service. The railroads responded by doing what they did best: carrying freight over long distances; in this instance the freight was truck trailers. Railroads were least efficient in terminals, but this element was turned over to the truckers. Truck companies simply drove the trailer to the customer once a train reached a terminal. To speed loading/unloading at these terminals, in 1963 Santa Fe put in service the first successful top-lift crane to remove piggyback trailers from flatcars. This arrangement helped spur growth in piggyback through the 1960s and 1970s. But railroads now also had to compete with long-haul truckers over great distances. To do so, they had to run trains that were at least as fast as trucks, and Santa Fe did just that.

In the mid-1960s Santa Fe's marketing department searched for ways to expand

the piggyback business of putting truck trailers on trains, now commonly known as intermodal freight. Santa Fe wanted to cash in on intermodal before air-cargo operators and shipping lines did. Cargo ship operator Sea-Land already was having goods placed in containers (trailers without wheels) for shipment across oceans. Santa Fe figured it was only a matter of time before containers began moving from coast-to-coast via the Panama Canal. The marketing people adroitly reached the conclusion that intermodal was the wave of the future for freight railroading, nearly 20 years before other lines caught on. Another group at the New York Central System was working on intermodal as well. The two groups concluded that there was a market

Santa Fe honored the nation's 200th birthday by applying a special Bicentennial paint scheme—a variation of the warbonnet design, of course—to five of its locomotives. SD45-2 5701, built by EMD in 1973, shows off its patriotic colors in August 1975. *Mike Schafer.*

RIGHT: Newer Motive power that formerly had served on Santa Fe passenger trains eventually became members of the freight diesel fleet. Two General Electric U30CG locomotives—once assigned to trains like the *Texas Chief*—ease their eastbound freight across the Rock Island tracks at Joliet (Illinois) Union Station one evening in 1973. The units have traded their red-and-silver warbonnet colors for the "yellowbonnet" scheme. *Mike Schafer*

Traffic was lean during the early days of the new intermodal *Super C* service. The eastbound *Super,* train 100, is at Winslow, Arizona, on April 26, 1968, with two locomotives and but a single flat car carrying two trailers. A new post-office contract would eventually fill out the premium-service train. *Bud Bulgrin*

for high-speed, transcontinental intermodal business and pitched management on the idea of a New York-Los Angeles joint operation. Test trains were run, and on one test the Chicago-L.A. run was made in 34 hours, 46 minutes at an average speed of 63.2 mph, setting a new record. This beat the time of the 1937 *Super Chief*'s record-breaking trip of 36 hours, 49 minutes. President John S. Reed, an early backer of intermodal, announced on June 1, 1967, that Santa Fe would inaugurate a 40-hour Chicago-L.A. freight service. The result was the fastest freight train in the world, the Chicago-Los Angeles *Super C.*

New York Central was hesitant, however, and dropped out of the partnership before regular service could start. Much of the business AT&SF had counted on was out of New York City, so the new train was handicapped from the start. A second problem was the high rate differential shippers had to pay to use the train, $1,400 per trailer, which was established in part to mollify freight forwarders who supplied a great deal of Santa Fe's trailer-on-flatcar business at the time. But President Reed still backed the idea, and it got underway at 2 p.m., January 17, 1968, as the first *Super C* departed Chicago's Corwith Yard.

The first *Super C* beat the record set by the test train the year before by making the trip to Los Angeles in 34 hours, 35 minutes. But traffic was slow to develop, and the train remained a disappointment until 1969, when the U.S. Post Office signed up for the service to carry parcel post (the department had canceled most of its mail contracts with Santa Fe in late

CHAPTER 4

1967). The train became more successful, but in 1976 the Post Office contract went to the Chicago & North Western and Union Pacific, and in May 1976 the train made its last run.

Nonetheless, the *Super C* had cast the die for Santa Fe intermodal operations, with service designed for what the customer needed—not what the railroad wanted to do. In 1968, the railroad carried 113,523 trailers; by 1972 this had grown to 156,262. In 1974, Santa Fe began operation of Chicago-L.A. intermodal train No. 188. It operated from Corwith to Hobart Yard in Los Angeles in 50 hours at standard intermodal rates. Next came train 189 between Chicago and Richmond, California. In 1975 came trains 199 and 991, which were scheduled to meet the requirements of a single customer, United Parcel Service, and also operated between Chicago and Richmond. Trains 199/991 were the hottest on the railroad after the end of the *Super C*.

The Post-Deregulation 1980s and Intermodal Growth

In the 1980s both railroads and truck lines were deregulated. The Staggers Act of 1980 directed the ICC to deregulate traffic when competitive forces would hold rates in check, and in 1981 it deregulated intermodal moves. Railroads could then offer intermodal service on any route at prices the market would bear. Competition became fierce, and cost-cutting became the order of the day. One dramatic cost cutter was the development of the doublestack car—two steamship containers stacked on top of one another—which allowed railroads to haul twice as many containers on the same train. Santa Fe began doublestack operations in 1985.

Another innovation was articulation—actually a reinvention of equipment engineering that began with early streamliners of the 1930s. In the 1960s most truck trailers were carried on 89-foot flatcars, but these are viewed as inefficient since the weight transported included a trailer's wheel assemblies—weight which in effect did not generate revenues. Further, piggyback cars tend to be more top-heavy which reduces ride quality.

To address these concerns, Santa Fe developed a "Six Pack" articulated car in 1976. This approach utilizes what is in effect a long, jointed railway car. Each Six

This eastbound intermodal train at Encino, New Mexico, in 1995 graphically illustrates the wide variety of intermodal equipment that would eventually be found rolling across the Santa Fe (and other railroads) come the 1980s. The first five "cars" are in reality an articulated car set, while Fuel Foiler cars follow immediately after. Farther back in the train, some truck trailers ride in a more conventional "piggyback" manner. *Howard Ande.*

Coordinated service between Santa Fe and Conrail grew to high levels in the late 1970s and 1980s. Utilizing Conrail's former-New York Central "Three I" Kankakee Belt line in north-central Illinois, east-west traffic could bypass the congestion of Chicago. In this view looking east at Schneider, Indiana, in 1981, a Conrail train out of Elkhart, Indiana, swings west off CR's Hammond-Terre Haute (Indiana) main line and onto the Kankakee Belt. At Streator, the train will enter the Santa Fe main line. AT&SF power worked as far east as Elkhart while Conrail power could be found in Fort Madison, Iowa, and even Kansas City. *Mike Schafer*

Pack comprises six semi-permanently coupled carbody units riding on seven sets of wheels, with each carbody unit carrying one trailer. The result is reduced tare weight and slack action. Santa Fe also built up a fleet of 10-unit cars based on this design, calling them "Fuel Foilers" because of their energy efficiency. Others followed Santa Fe's lead and articulation became standard practice in intermodal service.

Another development which helped Santa Fe improve intermodal service was a change in labor agreements. Even in the 1980s, crew districts were still only approximately 100 miles long, a practice which harkened to steam days when moving freight trains that distance indeed could take most of a work day. Better track and the advent of diesels allowed trains to make better times over the road, but the short crew districts remained. For example, in the 51 hours it took a hotshot intermodal train to travel from Chicago to Los Angeles, crews would be changed 17 times, with the average crew on the train just over three hours each time! New labor agree-

ments reduced the number of persons in the train to two, eliminated cabooses, and allowed crews to run through several intermediate crew change points, which helped reduce expenses and speed up schedules.

"Q" Trains of the 1980s

In a 1986 article on the *Super C* for *Trains* Magazine, former Santa Fe president Larry Cena remarked that the premium priced *Super C* was a good idea that came along too early, and there indeed would be a need for time-sensitive, high-speed premium service if you had the right equipment. Cena's prediction would prove to be true with deregulation, articulated and doublestack cars, and the new crew agreements. By 1986 Santa Fe was the premium intermodal carrier in the U.S., and was willing to again experiment with special services. It began an experimental intermodal service dubbed "Q" trains for "Quality Service Network." These new trains were short and operated on fast, frequent schedules to handle mail, parcels, containerized freight, and automobiles; they utilized smaller (three-person) crews on extended crew districts without cabooses. Initially the new service linked Phoenix with Kansas City and Denver with Houston. The hub for the service was La Junta, Colorado, with segments radiating from there. Cars from each of the Q trains would trade at La Junta before heading on their way. An advertising blitz even saw the railroad distributing free coupons to potential shippers to try the service once!

Although the QSN trains ended in 1990, a different type of Q-train service emerged involving longer runs. The longest was the famed Q-NYLA (for "Quality, New York to Los Angeles") which began service in conjunction with Conrail in August 1987, and became the hottest train on the railroad. Q-NYLA fulfilled the promise the *Super C* never could by offering true transcontinental service. Santa Fe had started down this road in the early 1970s with its "Land Bridge" concept, transporting containers which were off-loaded from ships in New Jersey and moved by rail to the West Coast, where they were placed on ships for Japan. Like the Super C, the Q trains brought precision, passenger-train-style scheduling to freight operations: in 1987 the railroad reported the Q trains had a 97 percent on-time record.

Santa Fe created an "intermodal business unit" to handle the marketing of the intermodal traffic. Many railroads were reshaping their marketing departments into business units, which segmented the traffic they were handling such as coal, automotive, iron and steel, and intermodal into business units. Following the deregulation of the rail industry under the Staggers Act of 1980, rates on trailer traffic began to crater. The intermodal business unit came up with an idea similar to one tried earlier with the *Super C* (and the *Super Chief*, for that matter)—charging an extra fare. It segmented the intermodal business into different levels and charged more for faster, premium service. If a customer wanted their trailer or container to its destination faster, they paid more for this service. If price meant more than time, then they could ship using a different, less expensive service. Service levels included "Q" (Quality or guarantee; this guaranteed that a Q train had priority over all other freights on the railroad); "P" (Premium); and "S" (double-stack). These symbols were contained in the alpha codes Santa Fe adopted to identify its trains, which helped

Short and sweet, a "Q" train burns the rails near Oklahoma City in 1987. The second unit out wears the "SPSF" paint scheme that anticipated the SP-Santa Fe merger plan that turned out to be ill-fated. *Steve Glischinski.*

THE TRANSITION YEARS

Locomotives stand at the ready at the fuel rack at Emporia, Kansas, in 1986. Rationalizations of one form or another were the rule in railroading during the last half of the twentieth century, and shortly after this photo was recorded, the office at left was closed as part of an ongoing strategy of systemwide consolidation of facilities. *Scott Muskopf*

operating personnel determine their priority. For example, Q-LAWS stood for "Quality, Los Angeles-Willow Springs" (Chicago). Shippers might be able to get a break on price based on the volume of business or the time of year they shipped.

With these new services, the railroad came up with a new way of judging its performance. It set a scheduled arrival time for every freight car, container, and trailer received and monitored it with special computer software. Using this "service scheduling," the company measured its on-time performance not on when a train arrived, but when the load met its pre-determined schedule. By the time of the BN merger, the biggest intermodal shipper was UPS, which even had its own set of train symbols. These were three-digit code numbers used for many years that were retained for UPS after Santa Fe switched over to alpha codes.

Santa Fe Mergers that Were . . . and Weren't

As the 1970s waned, the railroad merger movement began to pick up steam on a national scope—but with some caution. The disastrous 1968 merger of the Pennsylvania Railroad and New York Central, which resulted in the bankruptcy of the new Penn Central in 1970, and the bankruptcy of the Rock Island in 1975 and the Milwaukee Road in 1977 had caused railroads everywhere to put merger plans on hold. In the West the largest successful combination had been the 1970 merger of the Burlington, Great Northern, Northern Pacific, and Spokane, Portland & Seattle to form the Burlington Northern (BN also acquired the Frisco in 1980). But it would be a decade before another large merger was announced in the West.

On January 8, 1980, Union Pacific announced an agreement in principle to

CHAPTER 4

acquire the 11,277-mile Missouri Pacific (which by that time had actually become bigger than UP, which then operated 9,420 miles) for approximately $1 billion. MP lines stretched from Chicago into Texas and Colorado. UP followed up this announcement with another on January 21 that it also wanted to purchase the 1,482-mile Western Pacific, whose chief line ran between Salt Lake City and the Bay Area. Santa Fe had attempted to acquire the Western Pacific itself after SP announced in 1960 it planned to buy the road and merge it into its system. Santa Fe reacted by buying WP stock and developing its own plan to take over the smaller railroad. Ultimately the ICC rejected both the AT&SF and SP plans in 1965 and Western Pacific remained independent.

After Union Pacific's surprise 1980 announcement, Santa Fe—which for years was the only direct, single-line carrier between Chicago and California—was now faced with a larger competitor which could offer the same service, although MP provided UP with a roundabout route out of Chicago. Many of MoPac's lines in Texas served the same areas as Santa Fe, and the latter was none too excited about having UP in the Lone Star State. At one time the largest railroad in the U.S., Santa Fe would soon have more, larger neighbors:

Burlington Northern, which already was bigger, and an expanded UP. Santa Fe decided to take action.

On May 15, 1980, Santa Fe and Southern Pacific jointly announced a memorandum of intent to merge Southern Pacific Company into Santa Fe Industries to create Santa Fe Southern Pacific Industries. The two railroad subsidiaries would be merged to form the Southern Pacific & Santa Fe Railway Company. Santa Fe would be Number One in the new alliance: the company would be based in Chicago, not SP's San Francisco, and Santa Fe board members would outnumber SP's. An ominous sign even then was the quote from the chairman of the Interstate Commerce Commission that the proposed combination had "possible anticompetitive consequences." But there were other issues that apparently didn't sit well with the two roads' managements, and stories of internal conflicts arose. The two railroads announced they were terminating merger talks on September 12, 1980.

In 1983, the AT&SF-SP merger resurfaced, precipitated perhaps by UP's successful pursuit of MP and WP. On September 27, 1983, an agreement was announced that Southern Pacific Company and Santa Fe Industries would become subsidiaries of a holding company called

Crews of westbound train 195 hand their charge over to fresh crews at Emporia, Kansas, on June 11, 1986. Emporia was long a major division point, the first one west of Kansas City on the main line to California. Leading today's train is a unit in the merger scheme of the mid-1980s. Had the merger actually happened, the railroad would only have had to apply the letters "SP" between the "S" and "F" to bring everything up to date. *Scott Muskopf.*

Santa Fe Southern Pacific Corporation to "maintain our competitive position in an environment wherein major railroad combinations have taken place." This time each road got half the directors on the board, although Santa Fe would be 54 percent owner. The holding companies merged on December 23, 1983. However, the two railroads remained separate organizations and Southern Pacific Transportation Co., the railroad operation of SP, was held in a voting trust. Under law, the ICC had 31 months to decide the case after a merger application was filed. The new railroad once again would be called the Southern Pacific & Santa Fe Railway, a name which made up for in length what it lacked in creativity. While the two railroads weren't always physically close, they did serve much of the same area, making the proposed merger a "parallel" one—an issue which would become key in the decision of the ICC.

The last expansion of the Santa Fe occurred on December 31, 1983, when Santa Fe merged the 239-mile Toledo, Peo-ria & Western into its system. TP&W operated from a connection with the Santa Fe main line at Lomax, Illinois (with trackage rights into Fort Madison, Iowa), across Illinois to Conrail at Logansport, Indiana. The railroad, which served as a "bridge" line avoiding Chicago, had been owned 50/50 by Santa Fe and the Pennsylvania Railroad since 1960. In 1979 Santa Fe had obtained full ownership. Purchase of the "Tip-Up," as it was nicknamed, allowed Santa Fe to abandon its 58-mile Ancona-Pekin branch, the only Santa Fe branch line in Illinois. The amount of traffic that shifted to the former-TP&W line did not meet expectations and Santa Fe sold its ex-TP&W trackage in 1989. The new owners reinstated the TP&W name.

In 1985 the U.S. Justice Department came out in opposition to the proposed AT&SF-SP merger, while the Department of Transportation endorsed it. In the meantime, the two railroads began painting locomotives in a new common scheme with a warbonnet design but with scarlet, yellow, and black colors. New operating plans and a locomotive renumbering system was devised. As the companies awaited word from the ICC in March 1986, Larry Cena retired as president of the Santa Fe, and was replaced by John Swartz, vice chairman of SPSF.

On the morning of July 24, 1986, the ICC came out on the side of the Justice Department. It declared, in a 4 to 1 vote, that the monopolistic nature of the merger outweighed its public benefits, and denied the merger application. The fact that the railroads paralleled one another, rather than being end-to-end and serving different areas apparently weighed heavily in the ICC action. The *Wall Street Journal* described the rail industry as "stunned" by the decision. Some observers said SPSF stood for "Shouldn't Paint So Fast," referring to the locomotives being repainted prior to merger approval.

On April 13, 1987, SPSF Chairman John J. Schmidt resigned after four years leading the company, and was temporarily replaced by his predecessor, John Reed, who came out of retirement to take the job. Schmidt's resignation was seen by some as a result of how the abortive merger was handled. SPSF went ahead with an appeal of the ICC decision. On June 30, 1987, the Commission denied reconsideration, once

again on a 4-1 vote, despite SPSF granting extensive trackage rights to other railroads. The Commission further ordered that SPSF come up with a plan within 90 days to sell at least one of the two railroads, which then had to be done within two years. In July the SPSF board elected Robert D. Krebs, president and chief executive officer of Southern Pacific, to head up the holding company, with Reed remaining as chairman. Krebs had joined SP in 1966, and became president of Southern Pacific Transportation Company in July 1982. Faced with having to divest themselves of at least one railroad, the SPSF board decided to part with the less profitable Southern Pacific.

On October 13, 1988, Santa Fe Southern Pacific, which held SP in a voting trust, sold SP to Rio Grande Industries (RGI), parent company of the Denver & Rio Grande Western Railroad. RGI was owned by Denver millionaire Philip Anschutz, who picked up SP for $1.02 billion and assumption of SP's debt. After the sale, Santa Fe Southern Pacific changed its name to Santa Fe Pacific Corporation. After the merger disaster, the Santa Fe Railway was left heavily in debt. But in the 1990s the carrier would rebound and become, in its final years, one of railroading's great success stories.

High hopes for Chicago bypass traffic and traffic originating and terminating in the metropolitan Peoria area prompted Santa Fe to purchase outright the Toledo, Peoria & Western and later merged it into the Santa Fe system. Where red-and-white "Tip-Up" units once trod, two Santa Fe units roll westward through Fairbury, Illinois, en route from Indiana to Peoria. *Steve Smedley.*

Summing up the final years of the Santa Fe is this scene of an intermodal train out of the Bay Area crossing over itself at Tehachapi Loop in Southern California's Tehachapi Mountains. At the head of the eastbound train is an Electro-Motive SD75M—the last diesel series delivered to the Atchison, Topeka & Santa Fe before it was merged into Burlington Northern. The train is laden with the containers and trailers of J. B. Hunt Corporation, whose traffic—along with that of other trucking companies—boomed on the Santa Fe during the 1990s. *Marshall Beecher*

A "Super" Finish—Santa Fe's Final Years

1990–1997

Santa Fe's last years of corporate existence were highlighted by ups—better service, new trains, higher profits—and downs, such as employee layoffs, consolidations of facilities, and downsizing, although in the corporate world, if not for historians and employees, the latter are looked at as positives. In any case, Santa Fe went out with a bang, not a whimper, with "Super Fleet" locomotives that harkened to the railroad's "classic" period when red-and-silver passenger diesels streaked along with *Chief* streamliners.

Physical Plant Changes

As usual, changes and improvements in the physical plant continued in the railroad's last years. Early in 1990 a new diesel shop opened in Barstow, California, replacing a shop which dated from the 1940s. In March 1991 the last Santa Fe employee left the landmark Railway Exchange Building at 224 South Michigan Avenue in downtown Chicago, where the company had been headquartered since 1904. Some 350 employees made the move to a smaller but more modern office building at Two Century Centre in Schaumburg, a Chicago suburb, where rent was significantly less than that at the Railway Exchange Building. This was just one of the seemingly constant shifts of policy that resulted in employees being relocated, or in the worse case, laid off. Another example was the shift of Santa Fe's operating divisions.

Over the years most large railroads had set up "divisions" to oversee particular areas of the railroad on a more local basis. The manager of these divisions would report to a larger entity, such as a regional manager or operating department personnel at railroad headquarters. For many years the Santa Fe was divided into four "grand divisions," as the railroad called them. The Coast Lines were based at Los Angeles, the Eastern Lines in Topeka, the Gulf Lines at Galveston, and the Western Lines in Amarillo. This was reduced to three in August 1965 when the Gulf Lines were absorbed by the Western Lines. Each of these grand divisions was further divided into several operating divisions; in 1967, for example, the company had 16 operating divisions. By 1988 the number had dropped to ten, and in May 1988 this was reduced to six: the Arizona, California, Illinois, Kansas, New Mexico, and Texas divisions. At the same time, the grand divisions were reduced to two: the Eastern Region, based in Topeka, and the Western Region at Los Angeles.

This didn't last long: in 1989 the two regions were phased out, with only the divisions remaining. In August 1990, under President Mike Haverty's plan to streamline operations, the railroad was reorganized into four operating "regions:" the Eastern, based at Kansas City, Kansas; the Central, at Albuquerque; the Western, at San Bernardino; and the Southern at Euless, Texas (Fort Worth). Santa Fe leased new office space to house the regional headquarters at all but Kansas City. Expensive new dispatching centers were built into each of these regional headquarters. Haverty opposed the idea of a single dispatching center for the entire railroad, preferring to establish operating centers at regional headquarters to keep dispatchers close to their territories.

Container traffic became increasingly important as the century drew to a close, making the Santa Fe an integral part of the "land bridge" concept whereby intercontinental container movements utilize rail across land to shortcut what may be a circuitous all-water haul. In 1990, steamship line Maersk Inc. teamed with Santa Fe to produce a promotional film in which a Santa Fe EMD GP60M was painted in Maersk colors. The special train is on Cajon Pass on August 13, 1990. *Dan Munson*

All this changed again in April 1992. Santa Fe announced it was closing the four regional offices and consolidating operations. The change followed a trend of consolidation that several other railroads, including BN, CSX, and Union Pacific were following at the time. At Schaumburg, a new operating center brought in dispatchers from around the system under one roof, with the last dispatchers completing their move to Schaumburg on September 20, 1993. The new center also managed all equipment and track maintenance. At Topeka, freight billing, crew callers and customer service personnel moved into a central office. The company estimated the consolidations would cost $35 to $40 million, but the annual savings would be $14 to $15 million. Despite this fact, the consolidation caused problems for many employees who were forced to relocate.

With the regional offices vacated and operations centered at Schaumburg, it left a void in management on a local level. Consequently in mid-1993 the railroad was once again divided, this time into fifteen "operating superintendents" territories that resembled the old divisions.

Employees at San Bernardino Shops were also given the chance to relocate. On December 2, 1991, the railroad announced it was closing the historic complex, which by then was known as the San Bernardino System Maintenance Terminal. The shop machinery was moved to Topeka, ending 106 years of locomotive maintenance at the 60-acre California site. All 352 employees,

(down from 2,000 during World War II and over 1,000 in 1972) were offered jobs—if they were willing to relocate to Topeka. Not all took the company up on the offer, but for those that did their trip east began in 1992.

Topeka city officials had pushed for the consolidation of the shops at their city, and had offered tax incentives, job training, and low-interest loans for renovating Topeka's shop buildings. Their efforts paid off when Topeka Shops, which last had overhauled locomotives in 1949, once again became a locomotive shop in 1992. In the interim, Topeka had rebuilt passenger cars and was a major freight-car overhaul facility. When it returned to Topeka for locomotive work, the Santa Fe had come full circle: Topeka was the location of the first locomotive shop when the railroad was born, and it became the last locomotive shop when AT&SF was merged out of existence. The two other locomotive shops, at Albuquerque and Cleburne, Texas, were phased out in 1954 and 1989 respectively.

Other employees never had a chance to relocate if they were caught in the corporate downsizing of that period. Between 1990 and 1991 the work force was reduced by 20 percent: from 17,800 workers to 14,300.

The Return of the Warbonnet

All the previously mentioned changes were leading to low employee morale, and Santa Fe President Mike Haverty, a fourth-generation railroader who was making many of the changes, made a decision which would restore a measure of pride in the company: he decided to bring back the famous red, yellow, and silver warbonnet colors on the new Super Fleet locomotives being delivered. In a 1996 interview, Haverty recalled the decision:

"I was on a train in Albuquerque on a financial analysts' trip, and we had all these stainless-steel cars sitting there and two beautiful blue-and-yellow locomotives. As we stood on the platform I told Mike Martin [of Santa Fe's corporate communications department] the thing that is missing here is the red-and-silver locomotives. That is the best-known paint scheme, bar none, and a great marketing opportunity. I realized that, even though I was an operat-

Text continued on page 75

Santa Fe's famous UPS train 199 follows the serpentine steel trail through the Tehachapi Mountains between Caliente and Ilman, California, in May 1991. Precision service required by UPS meant an entire train dedicated to moving UPS-owned and leased trailers. *Brian Solomon*

The first locomotives to wear the red-and-silver warbonnet scheme revived in 1989 were the Electro-Motive FP45Us, which had worn the scheme when delivered new in 1967. Following the cessation of Santa Fe-operated passenger service in 1971, the warbonnet scheme was phased out and these and other red-and-silver units were repainted blue and yellow. On July 5, 1989, the 101 and mate make for a heroic scene showing off their new "old" livery at Cajon Pass. The revived warbonnet scheme featured huge "Santa Fe" lettering on the flanks rather than the smaller, black type they originally wore. *Alan Miller, Steve Glischinski Collection*

A "SUPER" FINISH

ABOVE: Trailers and containers of trucking giants Hunt and Schneider speed east through rural Illinois behind an EMD-GE locomotive combination at Ancona in 1995. *Steve Smedley*

ing guy at the time. I said to Mike one of these days I'm going to paint those locomotives red and silver. A lot of people didn't think that was too good an idea because it's pretty expensive to paint those locomotives. I figured I'd sit back and wait until the appropriate time.

"Once Homer Henry [then Santa Fe general road foreman of engines and a railroad fan] found out about my idea, he was bugging me about it all the time, but I told him to wait until I became president. Right about the time I became president, we were about to order 123 new locomotives—the biggest single order in the history of the company. Homer said if we were going to do this, then we'd have to tell EMD right now. So I said let's do it, and we made the decision. We still had the FP45s, so we painted those first. Everybody got all excited, and the amount of publicity, most of it free, was tremendous. The red and silver even came back on electric model trains, and pictures of the engines even showed up in Japan!"

The Super Fleet locomotives allowed the railroad to aggressively market Santa Fe's image of class, style, and quality. They were a huge hit, not only with employees but with the general public, and, of course, railroad fans. Their image graced magazine covers, billboards, the Santa Fe annual report, and videotape programs. The warbonnet made Santa Fe the highest-profile railroad in the country at a time when many railroads seemed to want to remain anonymous.

Haverty and J. B. Hunt

Haverty had joined Santa Fe in 1970 as a trainmaster in San Bernardino after serving several years with the Missouri Pacific; when he left "MoPac" it was the end of a nearly 100-year tradition of Haverty family members working for that company. At Santa Fe he moved around the system and up through the management ranks, eventually rising to vice president-operations. Haverty became president in June 1989 when John Swartz retired. At age 44 he was the youngest man to hold that position since William Barstow Strong a century earlier.

While Haverty is probably best remembered for bringing back the warbonnet, another decision had greater consequences

Is this the *Chief* or what? An all-stainless consist, including a Big Dome lounge, pulled by red-and-silver diesels made for a 1991 scene at Matfield Green, Kansas, that was remarkably similar to one that could have been taken a quarter century earlier. *Dan Munson*

Where conventional trains of mixed freight in boxcars, tank cars, hoppers, and gondolas once were common, intermodal trains are now the rule. Santa Fe intermodals pass in the daylight near Holliday, Kansas, in June 1993. *Dan Munson*

for the company's future business. In 1989, Haverty made a deal with trucking giant J. B. Hunt to move its trailers off the Interstate and onto the Santa Fe. Hunt had made the most of the deregulation of the trucking industry in the 1980s and had carved a huge niche in the motor-carrier industry by providing fast, consistent, and reliable service. Reacting to deregulation, many railroads dumped freight business they didn't want, which was happily picked up by new, non-union, post-deregulation motor carriers such as Hunt.

But in the late 1980s when these truckers went after business the railroads wanted to keep, most railroaders began viewing truckers such as Hunt as the "enemy." Haverty, however, saw great business potential in moving Hunt trailers long-distance. He invited Hunt to ride a business car with him on one of Santa Fe's intermodal trains. "When I was at Santa Fe," Haverty recalled in 1996, "I wanted to take people out on the railroad. We had gotten away from that. I wanted to take customers out. There is no better way to talk about your railroad than to get out there and let people look at it. At the time we had not fixed up our business cars; they still had 1950s decor, so we spent some money on them. We did this not without some criticism, because people said we were spending all this money on the train while at the same time we were cutting jobs. But the train was a great marketing tool—that's how I got J. B. Hunt. I knew if put him on that train I'd get him. I had guys come out there on that trip and hand wash and wax the locomotives. Hunt came out there and saw that train, and his eyes popped out!"

Haverty landed the Hunt business, and the new partnership was announced December 12, 1989. Service began in February 1990 under the name "Quantum." Santa Fe's role was limited to providing rail terminal-to-rail terminal service, with all other aspects such as pick-up and delivery, marketing, and fleet management handled by Hunt. Initially Hunt assigned 500 trailers to the Quantum service, which began between Chicago and Los Angeles. More loading/unloading ramps were soon established at places like Richmond and Stockton in Northern California. By April 1991 Hunt made its entire fleet of approximately 10,000 trailers available for intermodal service, and the service grew into Texas and Midwest points. The Quantum intermodal agreement with J. B. Hunt grew from 43 loads during the first month of operation to 4,412 in September 1991. Further growth put J. B. Hunt traffic behind only United Parcel Service as Santa Fe's largest customer (the Quantum name was changed to J. B. Hunt Intermodal in 1991). Subsequently Hunt established relationships with six other railroads.

Santa Fe to St. Louis

In March 1990 Santa Fe "expanded" in a sense: the company activated an agreement with new regional Gateway Western

For decades St. Louis was forbidden territory coveted by Santa Fe. Past attempts at gaining entrance to this important rail gateway were met with hostilities from rival railroads. Finally, in 1990, Santa Fe attained the city through an agreement with new regional railroad Gateway Western, which had taken over the former Gulf, Mobile & Ohio route between Kansas City and East St. Louis, Illinois. AT&SF power often ran though on GWRR trains, as on this westbound at the former joint CB&Q-GM&O depot in Mexico, Missouri, in the autumn of 1991.
Steve Smedley

Railroad to operate Santa Fe trains between Kansas City and St. Louis, a city Santa Fe had long been trying to reach. Under the "haulage" agreement with GWRR, the latter's two-person crews handled Santa Fe traffic between the two cities, usually with Santa Fe power running through. As part of the agreement, negotiated in September 1989, AT&SF agreed to route a guaranteed volume of freight traffic over Gateway Western to give it a reliable base of revenue.

Symbolic of the surprise merger announcement between Santa Fe and Burlington Northern is this scene—taken in 1996 after the BN-AT&SF alliance was sanctioned—of a BN locomotive seemingly eyeballing its mate-to-be railroad, represented by a GP30 rebuild, at Rochelle, Illinois. *Mike Schafer*

BN and AT&SF: The Romance Begins

A harbinger of the BN merger to come occurred in June 1989 when Santa Fe and Burlington Northern announced the completion of a Voluntary Service Agreement (VCA). The VCA called for coordinated marketing and operation of intermodal traffic between Southern California and Southeastern U.S. Under the agreement, Santa Fe handled marketing for eastbound traffic from Arizona and California to the Southeast, while BN did the same for traffic headed in the opposite direction. Domestic intermodal containers flowed freely between the two carriers, and sales reps from either company were able to sell single-line intermodal moves between points on the combined system. Haverty said at

the time, "Short of a merger, this is about the best you can do."

Events that occurred in November 1990 would effect Haverty's and Santa Fe's future. At that time, directors of Santa Fe Pacific Corporation (SFP)—the railroad's parent company (see previous chapter)—voted to break the company into three parts, spinning off the real estate and petroleum holdings as independent entities. SFP retained the railroad, Santa Fe Pacific Minerals Corp., and its interest in Santa Fe Pacific Pipelines. The company divested under pressure from primary stockholders Itel Corp. (which held 17 percent of SFP's stock) and Olympia & York (which held 19 percent), which felt the value of SFP's many parts wasn't sufficiently reflected in the company's stock price.

After SFP spun off its holdings in energy and realty, the railroad and holding company organizations were combined. President and Chief Executive Officer Robert D. Krebs headed up the holding company and Haverty the railroad. But Krebs background was in railroading, and that made for one two many chiefs, as it were. On June 5, 1991, Haverty stepped down in favor of Krebs; in 1995 Haverty returned to railroading as president of the Kansas City Southern Railway. During his tenure, the Santa Fe had cut its forces by 15 percent and reduced trackage by 1,500 miles.

Santa Fe Under Krebs

Following Haverty's resignation, Krebs became chairman, chief executive officer, and president. Carrying on the streamlining of the company begun under the Haverty administration, Krebs announced that $5 million had to be cut from budgets to improve profitability. The result was the elimination of 300 management jobs, who were "severed involuntarily" (a polite way of saying "fired"). More job cuts followed as the company cut personnel to the minimum.

Downsizing of the physical plant continued. System mileage was reduced, mainly through line sales, from 11,600 in the mid-1980s to 9,234 by late 1991, and to about 8,000 miles in 1992. Such line sales often resulted in new railroads—or the return of "old" ones. Such was the case of the Arizona & California, which returned as an

LEFT: Santa Fe's huge Argentine (Kansas) complex just west of Kansas City, Missouri, would endure as an important locomotive shop facility right into the BNSF merger. The same would not be true for such long-traditional Santa Fe shop locations like Cleburne, Texas, Albuquerque and San Bernardino.
Dan Munson

BELOW: Four GE Dash 840CWs wheel a Long Beach (California)-Kansas City container train through Crozier Canyon on the main line in western Arizona. Date: May 22, 1994.
Steve Glischinski

A portent of things to come: Burlington Northern Cascade green six and seven units back hint at Santa Fe's future (but not color scheme) as AT&SF SD40-2 5146 and its GE companions sail the up-and-down terrain at Winona, Arizona, in September 1995.
Howard Ande

independent company on May 9, 1991, when Santa Fe sold its old A&C lines to a limited partnership controlled by David Parkinson. Parkinson revived the Arizona & California name and hired Peter A. Briggs of Briggs Business Communication in St. Paul, Minnesota, to design a new paint scheme for the railroad. They agreed to use green as the primary color and, using a Macintosh computer system, Briggs laid out a striking combination of Cambridge green and smyrna (beige) paint which was applied to all of A&C's diesel locomotives. The new A&C continued in its original role, serving as a short-cut to California for traffic to and from Phoenix.

Shedding marginal track allowed the company to concentrate efforts on profitable mainline operations. During the 1990s the company exited its namesake city, Santa Fe, New Mexico, when the branch from Lamy was sold to Santa Fe Southern, one of whose owners is actor and railroad aficionado Michael Gross, famous for his role in the television series "Family Ties." The railroad also exited its historic trackage into Atchison, Kansas, in favor of trackage rights over other railroads.

Construction of new intermodal facilities were a big part of Santa Fe's capital improvement programs in the 1990s. On March 31, 1994, the first train arrived at the new intermodal and freight yard at Alliance, Texas, just north of Fort Worth. The new yard permitted the closure of an older, cramped intermodal yard at Zacha Junction, northeast of Dallas. On August 8, 1994, Santa Fe opened a new intermodal terminal at Willow Springs in suburban Chicago alongside a giant new United Parcel Service sorting facility. The new intermodal yard, adjacent to the Santa Fe main line, covered 269 acres and boasted four 5,000-foot ramp tracks which could accommodate long intermodal trains without switching. The tracks were spaced 108 feet apart to permit cranes to unload cars from either side. Yard tracks provide over 20,000 feet of storage space, with paved parking space for 2,900 trailers. The Willow Springs yard became one of Santa Fe's busier intermodal facilities. A new intermodal yard was opened at San Bernardino as well.

The Haverty and Krebs management teams made impressive strides with Santa

Fe. They took a company that emerged battered from the ruins of the Santa Fe-Southern Pacific merger attempt and turned it into a winner, albeit at the cost of many jobs. In 1993 Santa Fe had total revenues of $2.4 billion, with a net income of $338.8 million. It had become an attractive property—and it caught the eye of Burlington Northern.

While Santa Fe's management team was being hailed as one of the best in railroading, the same could not be said of BN. Formed in 1970 from the merger of CB&Q, GN, NP, and SP&S (and Frisco in 1980), the BN had consistently been profitable, but many on Wall Street felt that it was not living up to its full potential. In 1993 it had total revenues of $4.7 billion and net income of $296 million, its best profit since 1987 despite coping with floods in the Midwest—but still not up to what "the Street" hoped for. One of its failings was insufficient capacity to handle the enormous traffic generated on its lines, which resulted in train delays and lost business. In contrast Santa Fe concentrated on increasing

capacity: in 1994-95 it added 93 miles of new double track on its main line and more CTC as well. BN's specialty was moving coal and grain, while Santa Fe was the industry leader in intermodal traffic. A union with Santa Fe would produce a company whose commodities nicely complemented each other. BN would also pick up Santa Fe's management team: from the beginning it was obvious that while BN was buying Santa Fe, AT&SF would be the dominant partner. While rank-and-file employees probably trembled at Krebs' reputation for cost-cutting, investors and financial analysts were positively giddy about the prospect of a BN/AT&SF combination with Rob Krebs at the helm.

On July 16, 1993, the idea of merger was first discussed in a meeting between Krebs and BN Chairman Gerald Grinstein. At first they could not come to terms, with one holdup being Santa Fe Pacific's gold interests. BN had no interest in factoring the valuable gold subsidiary into Santa Fe's stock price for purposes of valuing the consolidation. Krebs pursued plans for

Three EMD and one GE cruising the central Illinois prairies with a westbound container train blow into Toluca on a fine June morning in 1996. The little burgh just west of Interstate 39 is famous for the three east-west avenues that lie to the north of the tracks: Atchison, Topeka, and Santa Fe streets.
Mike Schafer

The locals call it "Bill-Town," and the sports team is named the Bill-Town Bombers, but Williamsfield is what the Santa Fe calls this west central Illinois location of double crossover tracks. On this beautiful morning in March 1997, it still looks like the AT&SF as two types of horsepower from widely disparate eras momentarily share the spotlight in Bill-Town U.S.A. *Steve Smedley*

spinning off the gold company, and after receiving a favorable tax ruling from the Internal Revenue Service, it was spun off to SFP shareholders. Railroad merger negotiations resumed in mid-1994, and an agreement was reached. On June 29, 1994, the BN and Santa Fe boards met separately to consider the merger and approved the agreement. The formal announcement of merger plans came the next day, the same day the gold company was spun off. At that time, SFP's only remaining assets were the railroad and Santa Fe Pacific Pipeline partners. BN and Santa Fe expected shareholders to approve the deal, and receive formal approval from the ICC to merge.

But the two railroads had underestimated their main competitor in the West, Union Pacific. UP was not content to stand idly by while a new, stronger competitor was created in its backyard. UP Chairman Drew Lewis visited Krebs on October 5, 1994, and proposed a merger between UP and Santa Fe—and offered to pay a third more money than BN was offering. The BN deal was worth roughly $13 per share. UP

offered roughly $17 per share. Krebs reaction to Lewis' offer was unprintable, and his board of directors backed him up, saying the UP offer "is unlikely to achieve ICC approval and is motivated more by a desire to derail the Burlington Northern-Santa Fe merger than to achieve its own transaction with Santa Fe." UP went to court to try to force Santa Fe to deal.

Many on Wall Street thought all along BN's offer undervalued Santa Fe, and BN soon increased its offer to approximate Union Pacific's. This triggered another round of bidding with both companies slugging it out in ads seeking shareholder support for their bid. On October 30, 1994, UP upped its offer to $3.78 billion total, topping BN's October 27 offer of $3.2 billion. Santa Fe delayed the scheduled November 18 shareholders vote while the proxy battle progressed. Santa Fe also challenged UP to "put up or shut up." Citing the unlikelihood of ICC approval of a Santa Fe-UP combination (since the two railroads paralleled; a BN/Santa Fe combination was "end to end" and more likely to be approved), Santa Fe told UP it would consider UP's offer if UP established a voting trust. This would allow UP to buy Santa Fe immediately, with the two railroads operating separately until the ICC approved. Santa Fe shareholders would immediately be paid, with UP taking on all financial risk if the merger was not approved by the ICC. UP agreed to the trust idea, and Santa Fe continually delayed its stockholders' vote on the competing offers as it scrambled with BN to make a better deal. BN responded by matching the UP offer of $3.8 billion, and eventually had to raise its bid to close to $4 billion to ward off the UP threat.

On January 31, 1995, the battle ended when UP withdrew from the bidding after a Delaware Court rejected its request to bar Santa Fe from using "poison pill" anti-takeover measures it had adopted to ward off UP. UP took note, however, that its final offer had been 40 percent higher than BN's first offer for Santa Fe. Santa Fe stockholders finally met on February 7 and voted for the inevitable, approving the merger with Burlington Northern. The fight with UP was costly, but lucrative for stockholders: it drove the merger's value to Santa Fe stockholders up by 45 percent. The proxy fight would cost the company another $20 million, and drove up the merged companies' debt. But the merger was expected to save $346 million and boost revenues by $306 million.

It's open to debate whether UP was actually serious about acquiring Santa Fe, or if it just wanted to drive up the price for the competition. In any case, UP was shrewd—if the deal went UP's way, then it could expand its system and eliminate a competitor. If it didn't, UP would still drive up the price for BN. In either case Union Pacific came out a winner. In mid-1995 UP's attention turned to acquiring another Western giant, the Southern Pacific, which it succeeded in acquiring in 1996.

On July 20, 1995, the ICC approved the BN-AT&SF merger, and on September 22, the two holding companies, Burlington Northern, Inc., and Santa Fe Pacific Corporation,

merged to form the Burlington Northern Santa Fe Corporation. The new company managed both railroads as one organization until the end of 1996, with both the parent company and the railroad referred to as "BNSF." On December 31, 1996, quietly and without fanfare, the Atchison, Topeka & Santa Fe Railway formally merged into the Burlington Northern Railroad. BN then changed its name to the Burlington Northern & Santa Fe Railway Company. The new corporate logo retained the Santa Fe "cross" with the words "Burlington Northern" and "Railway" added.

So over 127 years of Santa Fe corporate existence came to an end. Through most of its life, the company had been managed conservatively. Profits were its Number One goal. But the Atchison, Topeka & Santa Fe Railway also took pains to present a progressive public image as it became one of the most successful railroads in North America. It could have painted its engines in drab colors, but chose the warbonnet instead. It didn't have to adopt the art and architecture of the Southwestern Indians in the design of depots, Harvey Houses, passenger-train interiors, and dining-car china, but it did. Its managers didn't have to use color, texture, and distinctive advertising to sell rail transportation, but they did. In a word, the Santa Fe had class. And that's as fine an epitaph for a railroad as can be written.

Aware of the extremely high recognition factor enjoyed by the warbonnet paint scheme, the newly merged BNSF opted to retain the colors for some of its new locomotives, changing only the flank lettering from "Santa Fe" to "BNSF." Meanwhile, the time-honored blue and yellow—a handsome scheme in its own right—was officially retired. This is Quality train QALLA (Albuquerque-Los Angeles) in Kingman Canyon, Arizona, in March 1996. *Steve Glischinski*

A trio of westbound streamliners strikes a classic pose at Kansas City Union Station on the afternoon of July 13, 1965. At left, train 19, the *Chief,* has arrived from Chicago. Out of sight at the other end of the station, through cars for Wichita, Oklahoma City, and Dallas are pulled from L.A.-bound No. 19 and shunted on to train 11, the Dallas-bound *Kansas Cityan* (far right in photo, behind E6A No. 13); similarly, through Chicago-Tulsa chair cars are switched to No. 211, the *Tulsan* (center train, behind E8M No. 83). Once the car shuffle has been completed, and steam and air lines connected and tested, Nos. 19, 211, and 11 will depart Union Station at 4:55, 5:00, and 5:05 p.m. respectively. *Mike McBride*

Passenger Trains of the Santa Fe

A SERVICE UNPARALLELED IN U.S. TRAVEL

As the 1930s dawned and the United States entered the Great Depression, rail traffic was on the decline. This was particularly true of passenger service, which suffered as more roads and highways were built for automobile travel. Few railroads in the U.S. had so firmly embraced the passenger train as the Atchison, Topeka & Santa Fe. From the time the railway was founded until 1971 when the federal government created a semi-private corporation known as Amtrak to assume the passenger-train operations of most railroads, Santa Fe was home to some of the most respected and famous trains in the country.

Early Services

Passenger service began on the Santa Fe in 1869, but it's first true "name" train was the *California Limited*, inaugurated on November 27, 1892, and operated nearly continuously until the mid-1950s (it was suspended for a time in 1896). By the turn of the century, the *Limited*, which operated between Chicago and Los Angeles in 68 hours, was so popular that several "sections" of the train were operated during peak travel periods—sometimes as many as seven sections of the *Limited* followed one another. A record of some sort must have been set when on one day 23 sections were operated westbound and 22 eastbound!

The *Limited* was known for fine service and top-notch equipment and by 1910 had received all-new equipment, including a two-car diner, club-lounge with soda fountain, a barber shop, and sleeping cars with inlaid woods and electric lamps of polished brass. An example of the amenities offered aboard the *Limited* was the practice of hav-ing uniformed boys come aboard the train at Cajon Pass outside Los Angeles, offering free boutonnieres for men and fresh roses for ladies.

Even the *Limited* was surpassed in luxury by the Santa Fe *de-Luxe*, which ran between Chicago and Los Angeles from 1911 to 1917 during the winter season. Operating once a week on a 63-hour schedule, the *de-Luxe* carried only 60 passengers who were pampered in every way. Passengers sat in wicker chairs and slept in brass beds, could look over updated stockmarket reports or read books from the library car, enjoy shower and bathtub facilities, or have their hair cut by a barber. An extra fare of $25—a steep sum in those days—was charged to enjoy the luxury aboard the *de-Luxe*.

Santa Fe enjoyed direct access to Grand Canyon National Park by way of a 64-mile branch from the main line at Williams, Arizona, to the doorstep of El Tovar Hotel right at south rim of the Canyon; the branch opened in 1901. To tap this market, in 1929 the railroad began operation of the *Grand Canyon Limited* between Chicago and Los Angeles, with through Pullmans handled right to the Canyon via a connecting train at Williams. At one time or another the *Grand Canyon Limited* handled through cars to and from Denver, Galveston, Oakland, Phoenix, and Houston as well as the Canyon. Always a workhorse for Santa Fe, a version of the train remained in service until the Amtrak takeover in 1971, although direct service to the Grand Canyon ended after the summer travel season of 1968. In 1989, the long-dormant branch to the Canyon was revived under the auspices of the Grand Canyon Railway (GCR). The tourist line,

ABOVE: In pre-*Chief* days, Santa Fe's most prominent train was the *California Limited*, a Chicago-California run of extraordinary popularity. One of Santa Fe's impressive Northerns is marching away from Wagon Mound, New Mexico with the westbound *Limited* circa 1940. *Railroad Museum of Pennsylvania*

which restored the Santa Fe Harvey House depot at Williams and the original 1910 Grand Canyon depot, offers an alternative to driving the congested roads to reach the park.

Other name trains which once graced Santa Fe's timetable included the *Chicago Flyer, Los Angeles Express*, the *Missionary, Overland Express*, the *Ranger,* and the *San Francisco Express*. Some local trains had exotic names, such as the *Saint* and the *Angel*, which during 1912-1918 operated between Los Angeles and the Bay area on a 13-hour schedule.

In the early 1920s the tourist trade to the Southwest and the Grand Canyon increased, and the railroad decided to offer other more economical services besides the *California Limited* on its Chicago-California route. The *Navajo* was inaugurated to serve the northern route over Raton Pass, while the new *Scout* mainly served the southern route via Amarillo and the Belen Cutoff.

The *Chief* and *Super Chief*

Santa Fe is probably best remembered for its fleet of *Chief* trains. Deciding that there was still a market for luxury service, Santa Fe drew upon on the Native American heritage of the Southwest when it inaugurated the *Chief* between Chicago

and Los Angeles on November 14, 1926. Operating on a 63-hour schedule, the *Chief* was the predecessor of an entire "tribe" of Santa Fe luxury trains. The original *Chief* was the last word in all-Pullman comfort and helped give rise to another of Santa Fe's many advertising slogans, "The Chief Way." The daily service, offered with a $10 extra fare, included Pullmans, a Fred Harvey-operated diner and club-lounge car, barber and valet service, ladies' maid service, bathing facilities, even a cigar store! In 1928, new buffet-library cars were added, and in 1930 the train was re-equipped with new Pullmans and three lounges. Running times were consistently reduced to 58 hours in 1929 and 56 hours in 1930. In the early 1930s Santa Fe air-conditioned the cars on most of its principal trains, and used the occasion to create new advertising opportunities. This helped boost patronage, but larger efforts would take place in the mid-1930s.

May 12, 1936, was an important day in Santa Fe history. On that date the railroad introduced what would become its most famous train—indeed, one of the most famous trains in the world: the *Super Chief*. Initially, the train was essentially a spiffed-up version of the *Chief*, using refurbished cars from that train, operating over the same route (but at different times of the day), and charging the same $10 extra fare. There were two areas where the new *Super* differed markedly from its predecessor, though: it ran on an incredibly fast 39-hour, 45-minute schedule (faster than today's Amtrak *Southwest Chief* over virtually the same route), and it was powered by new diesel locomotives.

The locomotives were designed and built by Electro-Motive Corporation under the supervision of its chief engineer, Richard Dilworth, with car-bodies built by St. Louis Car Company. Unlike later streamlined locomotives, the new locomotives for the *Super Chief* were box-like. The two locomotives, which together developed 3600 hp, were painted in blues, with an olive green carbody and red and tuscan separating stripes. The pair were dubbed "Amos 'n' Andy" after the popular radio show of the time. The diesel duo regularly pulled the *Super Chief* at speeds over 100 mph during the train's once-a-week round trip between the "City of Big Shoulders" and the "City of Angels."

Santa Fe Enters the Streamliner Era

The 1936 *Super Chief* was an immediate success, enticing movie stars and "high society" clientele to its Pullmans. But Santa Fe was already planning for a new version of the *Super Chief*. Lightweight, streamlined trains had been introduced by the Union Pacific and Burlington in 1934, and other roads soon joined in the streamlining craze as a way to attract passengers back to the rails. Santa Fe watched these developments with interest, and ordered an experimental streamlined coach, No. 3070, from the Edward G. Budd Manufacturing Company of Philadelphia. The 3070 arrived in January 1936 for testing. It had a fluted stainless-steel exterior, air conditioning, 52 seats, and weighed 77,000 pounds less than conventional equipment then operating.

Construction of the car used Budd's

BELOW LEFT: The *Super Chief* was one of the few trains in America that had its own china pattern—Mimbreno. It was conceived by designer Mary Colter, who also styled some Santa Fe depots and Harvey Houses. *Collection of Tracy and Dana Rice*

BELOW: The *Super Chief* was Santa Fe's first streamliner (see page 44 for a view of the first streamlined *Super*) and it was joined by an all-coach companion streamliner in 1938. Both trains remained first-rate operations right up to the end. Running combined, the two are shown descending Edelstein Hill (Illinois) in 1968. New Electro-Motive FP45 locomotives belie the fact that Santa Fe will be operating the trains for only three more years. *Mike Schafer*

patented "shotweld" process, which involved applying a jolt of high-amp electric current to the stainless steel, bonding the surfaces. Coach 3070 tested across the system along with coach 3071, also streamlined but constructed of heavier, Cor-Ten steel by St. Louis Car Company. The first streamlined, lightweight Pullman to operate on the Santa Fe was the also the first conventional sized streamlined sleeper, built in November 1936 by Pullman-Standard for use in the Pullman railroad pool.

In the spring of 1936, Santa Fe chose Budd to build an entirely new, streamlined *Super Chief.* Paul F. Cret, a Philadelphia architect and dean of the University of Pennsylvania School of Architecture, and John Harbeson, a professor at the school, worked on designs for Budd. Conception for the interiors of the train fell to Sterling B. McDonald, a Chicago designer-decorator who had worked on the designs of Union Pacific streamliners, and Roger W. Birdseye, Santa Fe's general advertising manager. Unlike any other train, Santa Fe

asked its designers to make the interiors of each of the seven passenger-carrying cars to be different—no two car interiors were alike.

Southwestern Indian art was employed throughout the train, as it would be on future Santa Fe streamliners. With the exception of a baggage car, all cars carried Native American names which were selected by Birdseye, an expert in Indian culture. The china used in the dining car carried an Indian motif from the ancient Mimbres tribe, created by Mary Colter (1869-1958), a designer, architect, and expert on Southwest Indians; she had designed depots and Harvey House buildings for AT&SF. Colter recreated 37 authentic Mimbres motifs for the china used on the *Super Chief,* which was made in Bavaria and became some of the most famous and most collectible of dining-car crockery. The diner was stocked with Irish table linens, and silver pieces by Reed & Barton and Harrison Brothers & Howson.

The new train would include eight cars, seven bearing Indian names: baggage

Boarding passengers have been seated but there's still some mail to load into the *Chief*'s RPO car at Galesburg, Illinois, circa 1955. It appears the engine crew of E3A No. 11 and its booster are getting a mite impatient. After all, this was an era when punctuality was the rule of the day. *Mainline Photos, collection of J. Michael Gruber*

CHAPTER 6

3430, sleepers *Isleta, Taos, Oraibi,* and *Laguna,* dormitory (for the crew)-barber shop-buffet lounge *Acoma,* diner *Cochiti,* and sleeper-lounge observation *Navajo.* On the *Navajo*'s rounded end was a drum-head-shaped sign in red and yellow with black accents on a royal-purple background carrying the *Super Chief* name. Externally the cars gleamed with stainless-steel car sides. Inside, Santa Fe and Budd designers employed exotic woods from Africa and South America extensively, with the exception of the *Navajo,* which featured copper-colored interior walls with Indian

other new Santa Fe streamliners. Even more special than these locomotives was the paint scheme applied to them by Electro-Motive illustrator Leland A. Knickerbocker. Many years later dubbed as the "warbonnet" scheme, Knickerbocker placed red paint with a yellow separating stripe around the nose of the diesel, with a portion trailing back on the locomotive flanks. The results resembled an Indian headress with feathers trailing behind. The traditional Santa Fe cross logo was modified into a stretched-out oval shape and placed on the nose of the locomotive with black "Santa

At the other end of the *Chief,* it was pure pleasure for first-class passengers, who could avail themselves of the observation lounge car which carried the train's lighted drumhead. *Railroad Museum of Pennsylvania*

sand paintings and a the ceiling done in turquoise. Specially woven carpets and upholstery with Indians motifs were used throughout.

To pull the new train, the railroad again turned to Electro-Motive Corporation. In contrast to the boxy locomotives built for the 1936 *Super Chief,* Santa Fe employed EMC's new E1-model passenger diesel—slant-nosed, streamlined beauties that could drum up 1800 hp to pull the new *Super* and

Fe" letters on a yellow background. The sides of the locomotive were silver. The colorful combination of red, yellow, and silver produced what most rail historians would agree was the greatest paint design ever applied to a diesel locomotive. Subsequently the warbonnet design was incorporated into thousands of model train sets sold over the next sixty years, making it one of the most recognizable paint schemes ever and garnering Santa Fe enormous free publicity and instant recognition even in off-line communities.

The new *Super Chief* entered service on May 18, 1937, and the era of Santa Fe streamliners was born (see page 44 for a view of the original *Super Chief* streamliner). On its pre-inaugural trip the train established a new speed record for the Chicago-Los Angeles run: 36 hours, 49 minutes, a record which would stand until 1967. In fact, the rail-searing run caused a traction motor to burn out in the E1 cab-and-booster set, so "Amos" and an experimental Electro-Motive box-cab diesel had to substitute on the first run.

In 1938 more new streamlined cars arrived from Budd and now also Pullman-Standard, including a second set of *Super Chief* cars, thus allowing twice-weekly round trips between Chicago and California. Six sets of new equipment went to streamline the *Chief.* Also included in the car order were reclining-seat coaches for an all-new economy service, the Chicago-Los Angeles *El Capitan*. While the *Chief* and *Super Chief* were the famous all-Pullman trains, *El Capitan* was Santa Fe's bid to win over passengers desiring less-expensive, yet comfortable travel accommodations. The train began operation on February 22, 1938, operating twice-weekly. The Budd Company built two five-car sets which were used on the 39-hour, 45-minute schedule. The trains departed Chicago on Tuesdays and Saturdays and from Los Angeles on Tuesdays and Fridays. Round trip fare was $65 plus a $5 extra fare in each direction. *El Capitan* was a hit, and in 1941 more cars were added to create eight-car trainsets. For postwar views of this train, see Chapter 3.

By 1940 a total of seventeen Santa Fe streamliner consists were in service. Four round trips a day were made by the Los Angeles-San Diego *San Diegan*, and between Wichita (Kansas) and Chicago the streamlined *Chicagoan* ran eastbound and the *Kansas Cityan* westbound. Operating between Bakersfield and San Francisco was the *Golden Gate*, and from Kansas City to Tulsa, Oklahoma, was the *Tulsan*. For a time, Santa Fe had more streamlined cars in service than Burlington Route, a pioneer in streamlined trains with its famous *Zephyr* fleet. Luckily, the explosion of new car orders arrived just in time for Santa Fe to handle heavy passenger traffic of the World War II years.

After World War II ended, Santa Fe bought more streamlined diesels from Electro-Motive (which had become a division of automotive giant General Motors) and purchased elegant PA-series stream-

lined diesels from American Locomotive Company. The PAs, with long noses and six-wheel trucks (wheel assemblies) wore the warbonnet colors particularly well and were dubbed by some the most beautiful diesels ever constructed.

Santa Fe placed orders for 156 new lightweight cars after the war, including 51 all-room sleepers. In September 1946 the *Super Chief* and *El Capitan* were increased from twice weekly to every other day operation, and the next year the *Chief* was dieselized and its running time reduced. A new innovation began in 1946 when the *Chief* began carrying coast-to-coast sleeping cars. Cars from New York Central's *20th Century Limited* and Pennsylvania's *Broadway Limited* from New York, and Baltimore & Ohio's *Capitol Limited* from Washington, D.C., were transferred to the *Chief* at Chicago.

New car orders finally enabled the *Super Chief* and *El Capitan* to become daily trains on February 29, 1948. On April 3 a new train, the Chicago-Houston-Galveston *Texas Chief* began operation, and in 1950 a new overnight service between Chicago and Kansas City, the *Kansas City Chief*, was inaugurated. During this streamliner era Santa Fe adopted its trademark "Chico," a fictional Navajo boy (page 38) whose image adorned timetables and advertisements. With great enthusiasm Chico extolled the wonders and delights of Santa Fe passenger trains.

To gain even more public exposure, beginning in the 1950s AT&SF sponsored the Santa Fe & Disneyland Railroad at Walt Disney's Anaheim (California) theme park, where the depots were adorned with Santa Fe's famous cross logo and steam locomotives were named for Santa Fe presidents. Also during the early 1950s, Santa Fe again re-equipped its streamliners, including the *Super Chief*. Between late 1949 and 1951 fifty-five sleepers, seven diners, an additional sleeper-lounge observation, and six dormitory-buffet lounges were purchased. The most luxurious cars to be added were six dome cars, which were introduced on the *Super Chief* in January 1951. Called "Pleasure Domes" by the Santa Fe, the cars featured a glass-enclosed upper-level seating area with swivel seats that provided passengers with all-around visibility. Below the dome was a cocktail bar; on the forward end of the car on the main level was a stylish lounge with a writing desk, and at the rear of the car and also on the main level was the "Turquoise Room," the first private dining room aboard a public train. Seating twelve passengers, the Turquoise Room could be reserved in advance for private parties. (This end of the Pleasure Dome lounge was always coupled to the dining car so that the Turquoise Room could be easily reached from the diner's kitchen.)

Santa Fe followed up the Pleasure Domes with the purchase of 14 "Big Dome" cars from the Budd Company in 1954. These cars had a domed section which extended the length of the car, with 57 seats and an 18-seat lounge. The lower level of the car, beneath the dome, featured a bar-lounge area. The cars were intended for service on the *Chicagoan/Kansas Cityan, El Capitan* coach streamliner, and the soon-to-debut *San Francisco Chief.*

The *San Francisco Chief* made its first run on June 6, 1954. The Santa Fe never had a direct through train between the Midwest and the Bay Area, although through cars had been offered, but the Chicago-Oakland *San Francisco Chief* filled

that bill. The train was assembled from a combination of existing cars (sleepers and diners bumped from the *Chief* and other streamliners by the delivery newer Pullmans and diners) and new equipment (Big Dome lounges and 48-seat coaches delivered in 1953). The new train was aimed at local and intermediate markets and, unlike most Santa Fe passenger trains, it operated via the southern main line and the Belen Cutoff. The train also handled through sleepers between Chicago and

Santa Fe operated a classic Art Deco passenger terminal in downtown San Francisco at 44 Fourth Street—miles from the nearest Santa Fe passenger train. Buses shuttled passengers between this location and Richmond, across San Francisco Bay, where trains like the *Golden Gate* and *San Francisco Chief* terminated and originated. The San Fran terminal is shown in July 1954. *Railroad Avenue Enterprises*

The *San Francisco Chief* is shown waltzing westward from Kansas City Union Station in 1966, not long after Hi-Level chair cars had been added to its consist. Inaugurated in 1954, the *S.F. Chief* was a late-comer to the *Chief* fleet. In modern times it was the only true through train on the AT&SF between Chicago and Richmond (San Francisco), although through-car service had long been available between those points via connecting trains west of Barstow. *Dan Pope Collection*

In 1957 and 1958, the *Super Chief*'s feature cars were redecorated, demonstrating Santa Fe's continuing commitment to the train. But on January 12, 1958, the *Super Chief* and its running mate, *El Capitan*, were combined into one train as an economy move. However, the trains maintained separate listings in timetables and in practice. Though run as a single train, their equipment remained separately grouped. During peak summer and holiday travel seasons the trains would operate separately, following one another across the railroad by only a few minutes as separate "sections." At the same time, the *Super Chief* lost its all-Pullman status—even when it operated separately, it often included single-level coaches.

During the 1960s as the U.S. passenger train network began to unravel at an ever-accelerating rate, Santa Fe continued to take a pro-passenger stance. It received 24 more new Hi-Level cars in 1964, one of the last large orders for new passenger equipment by a private railroad. These new cars went to *El Capitan*, with some of the original Hi-Level cars transferred to the *San Francisco Chief*. The company rebuilt and modernized sleeping cars into the mid-1960s, reduced off-peak travel fares, and offered special ticket packages that included passenger meals, and began accepting credit cards. Sales meetings touted Santa Fe's service and gave employees opportunities to make suggestions. The railroad continued to advertise its services in newspapers and magazines and on television long after other lines had given up the practice, and in the late 1960s purchased new locomotives from General Electric and Electro-Motive to pull its passenger trains.

But even these efforts couldn't stave off the red ink on Santa Fe's balance sheets caused by increased highway and air competition, much of it federally funded. In 1966, the railroad incurred a deficit of $31.9 million on passenger operations. The bottom dropped out in September 1967 when the United States Postal Service

Santa Fe served the Grand Canyon via a 64-mile stub-end branch off the main line at Williams, Arizona, where branch trains made connections with mainline trains. In the heyday of rail travel, many through cars destined to and from the Grand Canyon were switched to and from the branchline trains at Williams. In later years, through-car service ended and passengers had to make an across-the-platform transfer between trains at Williams (Williams Junction after the Williams-Crookton Line Change). In this 1968 view at Williams Junction, the eastbound *Super Chief* is connecting with branch train No. 14, at right with a single Geep, baggage car, and a coach. After this season, only buses will handle the connecting traffic. *Bud Bulgrin*

Phoenix, Lubbock, Texas, and Los Angeles, and another from New Orleans, which joined the train at Clovis. Additional sleeper-lounges were added in 1955. The *San Francisco Chief*, the last *Chief* to join the fleet, proved popular and remained in service until the advent of Amtrak.

The Hi-Level Revolution

In the 1950s *El Capitan* also received new equipment, including Big Dome lounge cars. But the popular train was destined to be the recipient of revolutionary new passenger rolling stock: double-deck coaches, lounges, and diners—the "Hi-Level" cars. Representing an entirely new concept in passenger-car design, two experimental Hi-Level coaches were built by Budd for testing in 1954. Passengers rode in the upper level, making for an exceptionally smooth and quiet ride, while baggage, restrooms, dressing lounges, and mechanical apparatus (such as air-conditioning equipment) were housed on the lower level. The new cars were extremely efficient, allowing almost twice the number of passengers to be handled in a single car with no sacrifice in space and comfort.

After testing, Santa Fe ordered 47 new Hi-Levels in 1955 for *El Capitan* service, including a lounge car dubbed the "Top of The Cap." The new cars entered service on July 15, 1956, after an exhibition tour which included off-line cities as far away as Washington, D.C. With the debut of the Hi-Levels, the *El Cap*'s Big Domes were shifted to the *Chief*, which by now was also carrying coaches.

ABOVE: An A-B set of E8Ms stands ready to depart Dallas Union Station with train 12, the *Chicagoan*, on the evening of August 27, 1967. When inaugurated in 1938, the *Chicagoan* and its westbound counterpart, the *Kansas Cityan*, were Chicago-Wichita trains with connections beyond to Fort Worth/Dallas. Eventually the pair were extended to Oklahoma City, then finally to Dallas. The E8Ms—rebuilt E1s—were regulars on this run. *Tom Hoffmann*

LEFT: Homing in on Kansas City Union Station on the last leg of its 256-mile trip from Tulsa, Oklahoma, the streamliner *Tulsan* hustles past Argentine Yard on an August afternoon in 1967. *Mike Schafer*

FRED HARVEY AND THE SANTA FE

Along the Santa Fe Railway in its last year of existence there were still elegant, Spanish-style structures standing near the tracks in places like Las Vegas, New Mexico, Williams, Arizona, and Needles, California. These buildings once served as luxurious hotels for Santa Fe travelers and were attractions in themselves. In addition to these were lunchrooms called "Harvey Houses" which could be found roughly every 100 miles along the railroad. These enterprises owed their existence to Frederick Henry Harvey, who founded the company which provided dining and hotel service to the AT&SF for nearly 100 years.

Harvey was born in 1835 in England and came to the United States at the age of fifteen. In 1856 he entered the restaurant business in St. Louis and three years later married Barbara Sarah Mattas. Harvey became ill, and his business partner made off with the money from the restaurant, so the couple moved on, eventually settling in Leavenworth, Kansas. Harvey became general freight agent for the Chicago, Burlington & Quincy.

As part of his job on the Burlington, Harvey traveled by train throughout the Midwest. At the time, railroad dining and hotel service were awful. In the West there were few, if any, dining cars. Instead there were meal stops at stations, where the food was often of poor quality. Passengers were overcharged and service was nil. Since stops were short, passengers usually had to rush through their meals, leaving food untouched (which in some cases was thus re-served to the next batch of rushed patrons). The profits from all this were divided by the restaurants and train crews. Box lunches and sandwiches were sometimes sold on board trains, but the quality of this food was no better than that served at station restaurants. Lodging was another problem for travelers as well as train crews. Rooms were often dirty or non-existent.

Having experienced all this, Harvey concluded there had to be a better way. In 1875 he entered into a partnership to operate restaurants along the Kansas Pacific (now part of Union Pacific) line at Wallace, Kansas, and Hugo, Colorado, but the partnership soon broke up. Convinced he had a good idea, Harvey first approached the Burlington, but it wasn't interested in getting into the restaurant business. Harvey then sought out Santa Fe superintendent Charles F. Morse with the idea of letting him operate one of the railroad's lunchrooms. Morse and Santa Fe decided to give Harvey a try.

In 1876 Harvey took over operation of the railroad's Topeka lunchroom. Under an agreement with the company which lasted to the end, Santa Fe supplied the buildings and the coal, ice, and water used in them at no cost to Harvey. It also provided transportation for Harvey personnel and materials, such as furnishings and food. All the profits went to Harvey, with Santa Fe in turn receiving fine meal service for its patrons. Harvey cleaned up the restaurant and expanded the menu. Business boomed to the extent that the restaurant had to be expanded. Santa Fe urged Harvey to open more lunchrooms farther west.

Harvey's first venture into hotels was in Florence, Kansas. In 1878 he purchased a restaurant and hotel on railroad property. Harvey sold the buildings back to the Santa Fe, then contracted with the railroad to operate the restaurant and provide hotel rooms for employees. An empire was born. As Santa Fe went west, so did Harvey. Another restaurant opened in Lakin, Kansas, and eventually lunch rooms and hotels were built at Newton, Hutchinson, and Dodge City, Kansas; La Junta and Trinidad, Colorado; Las Vegas, Lamy, Albuquerque, and Gallup, New Mexico; Winslow, Williams, Ash Fork, Seligman, and Kingman, Arizona; and Needles and Barstow, California.

In the beginning the hotels were set up just to serve Santa Fe passengers and employees. But after 1900, as many areas had become more settled, the Harvey company and Santa Fe began using the hotels and resorts to attract tourists for extended periods. Many of them were designed by architect Mary E. J. Colter, who would also design the china and silverware for the 1937 *Super Chief* streamliner. Colter used Southwestern Indian designs for the structures, which had Indian or Spanish names such as "El Navajo" and "La Posada." Her first effort was the Alvarado Hotel in Albuquerque, a huge adobe structure adjacent to the Santa Fe depot. Colter specialized in individual designs: the Harvey hotel in Santa Fe, the La Fonda, had 156 rooms for guests, but no two were alike. Hotels ranged in size from the huge La Fonda to The Havasu in Seligman, which had rooms for but 19 customers. One of the most famous and popular hotels on the system was the El Tovar located among the pines at the rim of the Grand Canyon.

Harvey House lunch and dining rooms were usually connected to the Santa Fe depot, allowing the restaurant to keep tabs on the progress of trains so that food stood ready as the train pulled into the depot. Harvey Houses would feed and lodge passengers and crews several times each day, depending on the number of trains serving the community. About half the Harvey employees were men, usually in management positions. Female employees waited on tables, and were dubbed "Harvey Girls." Young women were recruited from the East to work in the Harvey Houses, but according to Harvey's high standards, they had to be of good character, attractive, intelligent, and between the ages of 18 and 30. After a period of training, a Harvey Girl was sent west to their restaurant and lived in dormitories under the supervision of matrons who maintained strict rules. The Harvey Girls, decked out in plain black-and-white uniforms, were efficient and industrious and provided a stabilizing influence in the still-wild West. Estimates are that Harvey brought more than 5,000 women west. Many of them married Santa Fe employees and stayed to raise families. The 1945 MGM film, "The Harvey Girls" with Judy Garland, immortalized them.

"Meals By Fred Harvey" soon became synonymous with fine dining, and became another slogan used by the advertising department to entice travelers. While other railroads suffered under the poor reputation of their substandard lunchrooms, Fred Harvey's fine service and efficiency was bringing more patrons to the Santa Fe.

In 1888 Santa Fe began running dining cars on its trains for the first time, and in 1893 Fred Harvey received a formal contract from the railroad to manage their operations as well. At first, no dining cars were operated west of Kansas City, with trains continuing to stop at the Harvey Houses. But in 1892, when the *California Limited* entered service between Chicago and Los Angeles, dining cars went west for the first time. Santa Fe furnished the dining cars and Harvey provided the food and personnel. The railroad reimbursed Harvey for the losses incurred in operating the cars, which was every year they ran, since railroad dining-car service never was profitable and considered a "loss leader." On board the *Limited*, Harvey continued to enhance his reputation for superb food and service. Fine dishes served aboard the train included filet mignon, clams on the half shell, roast squab *au cresson*, and for dessert pistachio ice cream or strawberries and cream.

When E. P. Ripley assumed the presidency of the AT&SF, he was a strong Harvey backer and a new contract was drawn up which combined the diners, restaurants, and hotels into one operation based on a profit-sharing system. But Harvey was ill during much of this time, and gradually turned over operations to his sons and son-in-law. He died at the age of 68 in 1901, but the company he established carried on, as did his reputation for fine service to his customers. At the time, the company was operating 15 hotels, 47 restaurants, 30 dining cars, and even the food service on San Francisco ferry boats. Harvey also operated food services off line at St. Louis Union Station, and his company handled the food operations at Kansas City Union Station when it opened in 1914.

Santa Fe dining car menu from late 1960s. Mike Schafer Collection.

where chefs experimented with new and different menu items and a bakery was maintained. Other commissaries were at Bakersfield, Clovis, Houston, Kansas City, Los Angeles and Oakland, and there were additional points where trains could be restocked en route. For example, a chicken ranch and a dairy and soft drink bottling plant were maintained in

After World War I, during which the Harvey facilities were taxed to the limit, and into the 1920s, the Harvey system's noted service reputation continued unabated. One of the more famous incidents involving this reputation occurred in 1921. In Harvey House dining rooms men were expected to wear coats. The Houses maintained a supply of coats for men who did not have their own. In September 1921 the manager of a Harvey House in Oklahoma refused to seat a patron who was without a coat. The incensed customer was a member of the Oklahoma Corporation Commission and persuaded the Commission to order Harvey to drop the coat rule. Harvey appealed the decision to the Oklahoma Supreme Court, which ruled in its favor, and the coat rule stayed.

In the 1920s automobiles began to make inroads on Santa Fe passenger service, but on many trains business remained good. But the day of passenger train supremacy for long-distance travel in the U.S. was slowly coming to an end. In the 1920s, the Harvey company employed 5,000 people, but this soon declined as the Great Depression spread over the nation, forcing the company to retrench operations. As branchline passenger service ended, the smaller Harvey Houses closed. Many of the Harvey hotels were closed as well.

The late 1930s brought new Santa Fe streamliners onto the scene. Harvey was there as well, managing the operation of the diners on the new *Super Chief*. With the advent of World War II, the Harvey operations were once again strained to the limit. Employment zoomed up to 7,000, and many Houses reopened. The dining-car fleet was doubled and an incredible amount of food was prepared: on one trip of the *Scout*, 4,400 sandwiches were sold by Harvey "news butchers," and some dining cars were forced to serve customers in as many as ten 30-minute seatings for one meal. In 1945 the Harvey Company sold 5 million pounds of potatoes and served 20 million cups of coffee.

Santa Fe and Harvey once had a large and complex dining-car operation. The superintendent of dining cars reported to the head of Santa Fe's dining-car department, who in turn reported to the president of the Harvey Company. They managed an operation which stretched across the huge Santa Fe system.

To keep the Harvey reputation for fine meals untarnished, foods were carefully selected. The finest meats were carefully chosen from packing houses in Chicago and Los Angeles, and fresh fruits and vegetables from markets in the Midwest or California were shuttled to passenger-train originating points in refrigerated cars. The main dining-car commissary was at Chicago,

Newton, Kansas. Three laundries were in operation to keep linens and uniforms clean and starched.

After World War II, employment again declined. While some of the hotels in resort areas remained popular, others closed, as did many of the dining houses. In 1950-52 the *California Limited* began stopping at the Houses west of La Junta, but even reviving this old tradition could not save the eateries. In 1954 the company experimented with self-service dining concepts. "El Cafeteria" service allowed passengers to select the meals they wished and serve themselves, although a steward was available to carry trays to tables. Another experiment, used on the El Paso-Albuquerque *El Pasoan*, was the Lunch-O-Mat car featuring vending machines from which patrons purchased sandwiches, pastries, and refreshments provided by Fred Harvey.

Despite declines in the hotels and Harvey Houses, aboard Santa Fe streamliners Harvey continued to offer superb foods. One favorite of dining car patrons was Harvey's Santa Fe French toast. Even as late as 1960, Santa Fe and Harvey were serving close to a million breakfasts a year, and the most popular menu item was the French toast, which had first been introduced on Santa Fe dining cars in 1918. In 1963, one last innovation came with the introduction of the Champagne Dinner aboard the *Super Chief*. The dinner included complementary champagne and choice of entrees, which included such tasty items as sirloin steak or African lobster tails.

By 1968, with the huge reduction in Santa Fe passenger train-miles, the relationship with Harvey was deemed too expensive to maintain. On December 31, 1968, Harvey operation of Santa Fe dining cars was terminated, although the railroad maintained high-quality dining-car service under its own management until the end of Santa Fe passenger service in 1971. The Harvey Company itself had been sold to Amfac, Inc. in 1968.

Many of the old resorts fell to the wreckers ball, including the Hotel Escalante in Ash Fork and. most notably, the stately Alvarado Hotel in Albuquerque, demolished in 1970. But in the 1990s reminders of the great Harvey empire could still be found. The Fray Marcos luxury hotel in Williams was revived by the Grand Canyon Railway adjacent to the historic Santa Fe depot in Williams. Some Harvey Houses and hotels were converted into museums or offices, and at the Grand Canyon the stately El Tovar Hotel, remained the place to stay. In an interesting twist of history, thanks to the tourist-oriented Grand Canyon Railway, patrons could once again ride a steam train to the El Tovar. Fred Harvey would be proud that his dream lives on.

Both Santa Fe and SP offered service between the Bay Area and Bakersfield via California's Central Valley. Santa Fe's flyers on this 300-plus-mile route were known as the *Golden Gates*, one of which stands at Bakersfield on June 5, 1964, behind back-to-back Alco PA locomotives. Santa Fe bowed out of the market before SP, in 1967. *Bud Bulgrin*

informed the Santa Fe (and most other passenger-carrying railroads) that, as a result of the new Zip Code sorting system, it was discontinuing all but two of the Railway Post Office (RPO) cars operating on Santa Fe routes and that it was switching non-first class mail to freight trains to take advantage of lower rates. (RPOs were postal sorting offices on board specially-built cars.)

Santa Fe President John S. Reed called the action a "sudden, devastating blow" and combined with a big decline in passenger revenue that year, he was forced to take drastic action. On October 4, 1967, Santa Fe announced it would petition the Interstate Commerce Commission (ICC) to end all passenger service except the Chicago-Los Angeles *Super Chief/El Capitan* and connecting services to San Diego, the Chicago-San Francisco *San Francisco Chief*, and the Chicago-Houston *Texas Chief*. Of 39 trains operated by Santa Fe in 1967, it wanted to discontinue 33 of them. Among Reed's comments were "Santa Fe has not abandoned the traveling public—travelers show an increasing preference to fly or drive," which was certainly true.

Although many of the trains targeted were secondary runs, the petition included two famous trains: the *Chief* and the *Grand Canyon*. Ultimately the ICC gave its blessing to end most trains. Sadly, the *Chief* made its last run on May 13, 1968. The Big Domes thus rendered surplus by the

end of the *Chief* were moved to the *Texas Chief*, giving the latter train the best equipment it ever had. Interestingly, the *Grand Canyon* was retained and rescheduled such that it served as a Los Angeles connection for the *San Francisco Chief* at Barstow, handling the *San Francisco Chief*'s Chicago-L.A. sleepers.

The remaining Santa Fe streamliners continued in operation until the advent of Amtrak, the national passenger railroad, in 1971. Even then, with a tradition of over 100 years of passenger service, Santa Fe vacillated about joining the quasi-governmental railroad. Reed termed the decision to join Amtrak "... one of the most difficult that Santa Fe management has ever had to face." However, just ten days before the scheduled takeover, the railroad signed an Amtrak contract, and the last trains departed their terminals on April 30, 1971. The last regularly scheduled Santa Fe passenger train to operate was the *Grand Canyon*, which reached Chicago's Dearborn Station at 9 p.m. on May 2, 1971. Santa Fe passenger service had ended forever, and at the same time, Dearborn Station closed its doors forever to rail passengers after nearly a century of service (now restored, the depot remains as a handsome centerpiece to a new housing development).

However, remnants of the Santa Fe passenger era remain to this day. The railroad retained a set of streamlined cars for special operations, including a Big Dome lounge, and Amtrak purchased more than 400 cars, some of which are still in service. Amtrak's double-deck Superliner cars, in service on several routes including the Chicago-Los Angeles *Southwest Chief* which follows former Santa Fe rails west of Galesburg, Illinois, owe their design to Santa Fe's Hi-Levels. Several cars and locomotives have been preserved in museums, notably a pair of streamlined, bulldog-nosed F7 diesels at the California State

CHAPTER 6

The glamour and importance of the *Chief*s and *El Capitan* eclipsed Santa Fe's fascinating network of secondary connecting trains. Just one of several interesting backwater trains was No. 26, the Pecos Valley, a Carlsbad-Clovis (New Mexico) train that connected at the latter with the San Francisco Chief. This 1967 view of the train at Clovis reveals its short, but classy consist: Alco PA, baggage car, and observation car! *Tom Hoffmann*

Railroad Museum in Sacramento and completely restored diner *Cochiti* from the 1937 *Super Chief*. Also surviving from that train is observation car *Navajo* at the Colorado Railroad Museum in Golden. Most of the Big Dome cars remain in service, working in "cruise train" service on the Alaska Railroad. Eighteen years after the Amtrak takeover, the famous warbonnet passenger colors were revived by Santa Fe for use on freight diesels. The warbonnet livery survives as one of the color schemes of the new Burlington Northern & Santa Fe Railway, carrying on the rich tradition of the once-great fleet of *Chief*s and their brethren.

Another obscure local train was Nos. 13 and 14 between Albuquerque and El Paso, 253 miles. Northbound 14 is making its station call at Las Lunas, New Mexico, between Albuquerque and Belen on March 30, 1968. The train served as a connection to the *S. F. Chief* at Belen and the *Super Chief* and El *Capitan* at Albuquerque. Budd Rail Diesel Cars are serving on this day's run. *Ernest Robart, Bud Bulgrin Collection*

After an absence of nearly 35 years, steam returned to Santa Fe rails early in the 1990s when the railroad's first 4-8-4, the 3751 (also builder Baldwin's first 4-8-4), was resurrected by the San Bernardino Historical Society with help from AT&SF. The Northern's most ambitious outing was a round trip from Los Angeles to Chicago during the summer of 1992 utilizing Santa Fe passenger equipment that had been retained by the railroad. Assisted by two new Santa Fe GE diesels, the special arrives at Chillicothe, Illinois (the first division point out of Chicago), on its return trip to California to the delight of hundreds of people, many from nearby Peoria. *Steve Smedley*

Santa Fe's Steam Fleet

LOCOMOTIVES THAT MOVED AT&SF TRAINS FROM 1868 TO 1957

The Atchison, Topeka & Santa Fe had a history of providing fine steam power to pull its trains. From the diminutive 4-4-0 "American"-type locomotives of the nineteenth century to giant 2-10-4 "Texas" types of the 1940s, Santa Fe steam power was second to none.

The Early Years

The first steam locomotive on the Santa Fe was purchased on March 31, 1869. The locomotive, a 4-4-0 , was obtained from the Ohio & Mississippi Railroad, a broad-gauge (standard gauge in the U.S. being 4-8½ inches) line. It was built by the Niles Machine Works of Cincinnati, Ohio, and after being re-gauged and delivered to the company was numbered 1 and named *Cyrus K. Holliday* after the Santa Fe's founder. This locomotive burned coal, but the next to arrive, built in 1869 by the Rhode Island Locomotive Works, burned wood. It turned out to be a less reliable machine than No. 1. Also in 1869 came engine No. 3, named *Dauntless* and built by the Taunton (Massachusetts) Locomotive Works. It was purchased second-hand from the Boston, Hartford & Erie Railroad. These three engines were the earliest examples of what would be 88 years of Santa Fe steam power.

Between 1870 and 1872 the railroad placed orders for 36 more American types to service the expanding system. By 1877, 60 locomotives were on the property, all of them American types except for four locomotives used in switching service. These engines were serviced by the shops at Topeka, which, ironically enough, was the same location of Santa Fe's last locomotive shop at the end of its corporate existence when the company merged with Burlington Northern at the end of 1996. Topeka also built locomotives, including a 4-4-0 also named for Cyrus K. Holliday, another locomotive named for William B. Strong, and a third produced in 1882 with the name *T. C. Wheeler*. That same year the company discontinued the practice of naming locomotives.

In 1880 Santa Fe purchased its made its first purchase of 2-6-0s, called "Moguls," followed by five more in 1881. Also coming were Ten-Wheelers with the 4-6-0 wheel arrangement. As the road pushed west and faced mountain grades, larger locomotives were required. The first 2-8-0 locomotive, named *Uncle Dick*, came in 1878 to aid in the construction of the line over Raton Pass. Beginning in 1881, the Baldwin Locomotive Works, Brook Works, and Pittsburgh Locomotive built a fleet of 2-8-0s for Santa Fe, and they became the backbone of the early fleet, which by 1881 had reached 233 steam locomotives.

Post-1900 Steam

Mikados (2-8-2s) and Decapods (2-10-0s): By the turn of the century the era of modern steam power was underway. Heavy locomotives of the 2-8-2—or Mikado—wheel arrangement made their debut, and three 2-10-0s (Decapods), designed for use as helpers on mountain grades arrived in 1902. The first of these was built by Baldwin and the second two by American Locomotive. At the time of their

Named for one of Santa Fe's founding fathers, the *Wm. B. Strong*—engine No. 2—was one of the first locomotives built by Topeka Shops. The 4-4-0 is shown circa 1881. *Railroad Museum of Pennsylvania*

construction they were the largest and most powerful locomotives in the world. All three were initially used on Raton Pass, helping trains over the steep grades. The three Decapods ended up being the precursors of what became known as the 2-10-2 Santa Fe-type.

In 1929 eight more Decapods came to the Santa Fe, not through a new order but with the purchase of the Kansas City, Mexico & Orient. They had interesting histories: they were built for use in Russia, but the revolution in that country in 1917 resulted in them being held in the United States. The USRA gained control of them and put the engines to work across the U.S. Three of the engines were scrapped almost immediately by the AT&SF, but the other five, numbered in Santa Fe's 2565 class, stayed on the property until 1955 when they were scrapped.

"Santa Fe" type—2-10-2s: The 2-10-2 Santa Fe types designed in conjunction with the Baldwin Locomotive Works in 1903 were descendants of the Decapods, the 2-10-0s. A rear trailing truck was installed to help provide a guide for reverse movements, as well as to support a larger firebox. Helper engines spent a lot of their time going backward, particularly on Cajon and Raton passes, and locomotive flexibility greatly increased if an engine could sim-

ply back up rather than using a turntable or wye to turn around. Thus the Santa Fe type was born, and eventually 332 of these workhorse engines were purchased: 71 were ordered in 1903, 15 in 1904, 74 in 1905 (which were delivered over a two-year period), and 32 more in 1912-13. More modern Santa Fes came between 1919 and 1927, when 140 members of the 3800 class joined the roster. These locomotives had longer wheelbases which could handle curves better, and 200-pound boiler pressure for increased power. But the engines also proved to be maintenance headaches and had to be rebuilt, after which they went on to provide many years of reliable service for their namesake railroad.

Atlantics (4-4-2s) and Pacifics (4-6-2s): For passenger service, speedy 4-4-2 Atlantics and 4-6-2 Pacific types were purchased. The 4-4-2s, while not the most powerful of steam locomotive, could blister the rails. The four-wheel leading truck helped tracking ability, and the trailing truck allowed for larger boilers which steamed well. Santa Fe received the second Atlantic ever built in September 1889, and eventually accumulated 183 examples of the type.

Even more popular with railroads across the land was the 4-6-2 Pacific type, of which Santa Fe acquired 274. The Pacific was well accepted by nearly every railroad worth its salt, and it became the standard passenger locomotive during the early years of the twentieth century. Santa Fe was no exception, and acquired 274 Pacifics between 1903 and 1924. Until the arrival of more powerful engines, the Pacifics reigned supreme in passenger service. Many were upgraded over the years with larger drivers and other modifications, and they provided excellent service to the company right to the end. Six examples of the Pacific type were saved. Number 1316, which had been on display in San Angelo, Texas, was moved in 1980 to the Texas State Railroad at Rusk and restored to service as Texas State No. 500 in 1981. It remains in service today pulling tourist passenger trains.

Mallets, articulateds, and experimentals: Santa Fe wasn't afraid to experiment in an effort to produce larger engines to pull heavier trains. In 1911, Topeka Shops converted ten 2-10-2s into huge 2-10-10-2 Mallet types. However, the rebuild was not successful, and the engines were returned to their original wheel arrangement between 1915 and 1918. Santa Fe also had a number of 2-6-6-2 Mallets on their roster, but unlike its Western neighbors, the Mallets never caught on with AT&SF.

During World War II when traffic levels were at their peak, eight used Class Y-3 2-

8-8-2s were purchased from the Norfolk & Western Railway. Built by Alco in 1919, they were numbered 1790-1797. The big engines only worked three years on Raton Pass grades before seven were sold to the Virginian Railway in 1948 (the other Mallet was scrapped at Albuquerque). One interesting aside of the ex-N&W Mallet story was that the mechanical department considered using their boilers to upgrade some of the 3751-class 4-8-4s built in the 1920s, but the idea was dropped when the engines were sold to the Virginian.

Another Santa Fe experiment was attempted in 1919 under the direction of Assistant to Vice President–Mechanical John Purcell. He headed up Santa Fe's mechanical department beginning in 1912 and would remain in that capacity until 1941. In 1919 he ordered one of the 2-10-2s being built by Baldwin, No. 3829, to be equipped with a four-wheel truck. Technically, this was the first example of the 2-10-4 design, but it was considered experimental and Baldwin termed it a 3800 class "modified."

Mountains (4-8-2s): A combination of the features of the Pacific (4-6-2) and Mikado (2-8-2) designs resulted in the 4-8-2 Mountain type. It was originally used on mountain grades by the Chesapeake & Ohio, and the first examples came to the Santa Fe in 1918. They were ideally suited

The Mikado-type locomotive—the 2-8-2—was popularized during the World War I era and commonly found on railroads throughout the land. The 4103, shown at Tulsa, Oklahoma, was a 1927 of Baldwin Locomotive Works. *Bud Bulgrin Collection*

In steam-locomotive history, Santa Fe was arguably best known for the development of the "Santa Fe"-type, the 2-10-2, represented by the 3803 at Kansas City, Kansas. The railroad simply took the Decapod type (the 2-10-0, widely used on the Pennsylvania Railroad's mountainous routes) and added one set of trailing wheels for added support of an enlarged firebox. Like its 2-10-0 cousin, the 2-10-2 was ideal for the rigors of mountain railroading. *Bud Bulgrin Collection*

to Santa Fe service, as they had large cylinders, big boilers and high tractive effort to pull trains over the mountains or step out on the plains. More power was needed not only for the mountains, but trains were getting heavier, too. The advent of all-steel cars made passenger trains heavier than the wood and steel-sheathed wood cars that came before. The first of the Mountains was ordered in March 1917. Number 3700 was a coal burner, but the next locomotive to follow, 3701, burned oil. Both arrived in 1918, and were followed by oil burners 3702-3706 and coal burners 3707-3711. All were in service in 1919.

More Mountains followed in 1920-22, and a final order for Nos. 3745-3750 was placed in January 1924. They headed up many of Santa Fe's famous name trains, including the *California Limited*, the *Grand Canyon*, and the *Fast Mail*, and secondary trains such as the Denver-La Junta *Centennial State*. In the 1930s, as 4-8-4 Northern types arrived and train schedules were speeded up, the 4-8-2s were knocked down to secondary runs and freight service and in World War II handled troop trains. The last of these majestic engines was sold for scrap in 1955.

The "Big Three"

In the year 1920 steam power reached its zenith on the Santa Fe, with 2,195 locomotives owned, but its most famous steam engines had yet to arrive. These were the 4-6-4, 4-8-4, and 2-10-4 types, dubbed the "Big Three" by author S. Kip Farrington Jr. in his 1972 book on these locomotives. The Big Three were modern machines in every way, with plenty of power, large tenders for longer runs, and interchangeable parts to cut down on maintenance. At one time they averaged 9,000 revenue-miles per month in passenger service and 6,000 miles a month in freight service. They were locomotives of big accomplishments. John S. Reed, long-time president of the Santa Fe who worked on crews testing steam and diesel locomotives in the late 1930s, called the newer 4-8-4s and 2-10-4s the "...finest that were built from either a theoretical design or practical performance standpoint" in a 1974 letter to *Trains* Magazine.

Hudsons (4-6-4s): The 4-6-4 was named the "Hudson" after the river in New York which paralleled the lines of the first railroad to use the type, the New York Central. Santa Fe was an early user of the Hudson,

We're on a footbridge over San Bernardino Yard in April 1947 for a down-on look at 2-10-2 No. 3860 on a freight "Extra." The Santa Fe types were well-suited for getting trains over Cajon Pass just east of San Bernardino. *Bud Bulgrin Collection*

with ten arriving in 1927 only 90 days after the first of the type were built for NYC. Numbered in the 3450 class, these engines pushed aside the Pacifics on passenger runs. They were equipped with 73-inch drivers. Beginning in the 1930s they were rebuilt with higher boiler pressures and wider 79-inch drivers, which increased performance considerably. They spent much of their lives working between Kansas City and La Junta and Kansas City and Clovis on trains such as the *Colorado Flyer*, the *Navajo*, the *Missionary*, and the *Scout* in addition to more famous trains.

The 3450 class was the precursor to six larger Hudsons which arrived in 1937 from Baldwin Locomotive Works. Equipped with 84-inch drivers, 300 pounds of boiler pressure (although designed for 310 pounds). They were oil burners whose tenders carried 20,000 gallons of water and 7,000 gallons of oil and had big six-wheel trucks to support them. The 3460 class 4-6-4s were assigned to the territory between Chicago and La Junta, a distance of about 1,000 miles where there were few grades and the locomotives could move passenger trains at high speed. The 3460s were record-setters, too. One engine set the record for the longest continuous run ever made by a steam locomotive in regular passenger service.

That record-setting locomotive was No. 3461. It was received by Santa Fe at Shopton (the shops at Fort Madison, Iowa) on October 29, 1937. The new engine made its first break-in run on a 57-car extra freight from Shopton to Chillicothe, Illinois, on November 5, 1937, departing eastbound at 11:52 a.m. Its first passenger run was made on November 17, 1937, when it left Chicago westbound on train 15 with 11 cars at 1:57 a.m., arriving at Shopton at 7:19 a.m.

On December 9, 1937, 3461 departed Los Angeles (along with helper 1371 which was dropped off at Upland, California) at 11:02 p.m. with train No. 8, the *Fast Mail*. Fifty-three hours and forty minutes later, on December 12, 1937, the train pulled into Chicago's Dearborn Station—behind the same locomotive! (This was in an era when a train's steam locomotive was changed at nearly every division point.) Pulling ten to twelve passenger cars, the 3461 had made the entire 2,227-mile run

to Chicago without change. Helper engines were added at six additional points, oil was taken on at five points, and water 18 times.

One member of the class, No. 3460, received a huge streamlined shroud to pull the newly streamlined *Chief* and was painted two-tone blue with stainless steel trim; the one-of-kind streamlined Hudson thus earned the nickname "Blue Goose." It was the only fully streamlined steam locomotive the railroad ever operated. Fittingly, one member of this class, No. 3463, was selected for preservation at the birthplace of the Santa Fe, Topeka.

Northerns (4-8-4s): Another member of the Big Three was the 4-8-4 or Northern type, named for the first railroad to purchase that wheel arrangement, the Northern Pacific. In the mid-1920s, growing consists led Santa Fe to focus on the purchase of heavier passenger power, particularly for use west of La Junta to Albuquerque, where passenger trains had to wrestle with Raton and Glorieta passes. Mechanical engineer H. H. Lanning worked with the Baldwin Locomotive Works on the design of Santa Fe's first Northerns, which were assigned in the 3751-class. Locomotive 3751 was delivered in May 1927 and was the first of what would grow to a fleet of 65 Northerns on the railroad. It received extensive testing, comparing its performance against 4-8-2 No. 3714. The new engine could pull 33% more freight than the 3714 using 19% less coal, and could pull nine passenger cars over Raton Pass without a helper engine.

The next nine members of the 3751-class arrived in January and February 1928. All ten locomotives, which were coal burners, went into service over the New Mexico Division between La Junta and Albuquerque. They handled the majority of the passenger assignments between the two points, bumping 4-8-2s off those runs. In April 1929 four more locomotives, Nos. 3761-3764, were received. The engines joined their sisters in working La Junta-Albuquerque, plus ran through to Winslow and east to Clovis.

Despite their superior performance over other, smaller engines, the 3751-class did not develop as much power as the company hoped for. The reason was that the large cylinders on the front of the engine, which were 30 inches in diameter, created a high

back pressure at speed which reduced their power. In November 1936 eleven new 4-8-4s were ordered, but this time smaller cylinders were part of the design, and the oil-burning locomotives would have bigger 80-inch driving wheels and the boiler pressure increased to 300 pounds for more power. Dubbed the 3765 class, the new engines arrived in 1938. The new engines were able to run all the way through from La Junta across mountain and desert to Los Angeles, a trip of 1,235 miles with grades up to 3.5 percent. In the meantime the 14 members of the 3751 class were converted to oil burners by the Albuquerque shops and received bigger tenders which had a capacity of 20,000 gallons of water and 7107 gallons of fuel oil, the same type of tender used on the 3765 class. Once converted to oil, the 3751 class' territory was also extended to allow them to run all the way from La Junta to Los Angeles.

Between 1938 and 1941 all the 3751-class engines were rebuilt at Albuquerque with larger driving wheels, roller bearings,

a lengthened wheelbase, air pumps on the pilot deck, and longer smokeboxes. This and other modifications changed their appearance and improved performance. The first engine completed was the 3753 on November 11, 1938. Beginning in 1940, the 3751s were allowed to handle the *Grand Canyon* between Wellington, Kansas, and Los Angeles—at 1,534 miles the longest steam-locomotive run on the system. In 1941, ten more 4-8-4s came to the Santa Fe, designated the 3776-class. They were essentially the same as the 3765-class, except they had larger tenders. Their first assignments were on the *Chief, Fast Mail,* and *California Limited* between La Junta and Los Angeles. With the onset of World War II, locomotive operating districts were extended, and some of the Northerns handled passenger trains all the way from Kansas City to Los Angeles, 1,775 miles!

A new class of 4-8-4 came to the Santa Fe during the war. Between November 1943 and March 1944, 30 new 4-8-4s, this time in the 2900-class and numbered

Pacifics (4-6-2s) were very common on railroads throughout North America and were principally used on passenger trains. Pacifics 1263 and 3445 double-head a head-end heavy passenger train on the Central Valley line at Pinole, California, just outside of Richmond. The grades between the Bay Area and Stockton sometimes required supplemental locomotives. *Arthur B. Johnson, Bud Bulgrin Collection*

Santa Fe partially streamlined two Pacifics, the 1369 (above, at Oakland, in 1940) and 1376 for use on the *Valley Flyer*, a short-lived Oakland-Bakersfield train inaugurated for the 1939 World's Fair at San Francisco. *Railroad Museum of Pennsylvania*

2900-2929, arrived to work in fast freight service between Kansas City and Clovis. These were duplicates of the 3776-class, although they weighed more due to wartime material restrictions, becoming the heaviest 4-8-4s ever built. They probably would never would have been ordered if World War II had not prevented the delivery of more diesel locomotives, but they were fine machines, capable of developing 5600 hp at speeds above 40 mph. They were the last passenger steam locomotives purchased by the Santa Fe, but were used in freight service as well. The 30 engines in the 2900 class received Timken roller bearing side rods in 1947-48.

By 1949 the 3776 class 4-8-4s were mainly in freight service between Kansas City and Clovis, displaced by diesels on passenger runs. The last 3751-class engine to run operated in 1955, but several members of the other 4-8-4 classes made runs into the mid-1950s. By 1957 two 4-8-4s, the 2907 and 3780, were the last of their type running, reduced to helper service out of Belen, New Mexico. The 3780, which had received a new boiler in 1952, was the last steam engine to operate on the Santa Fe system.

"Texas" type (2-10-4): Texas"types of the 2-10-4 wheel arrangement were the third member of the Santa Fe's trio of superior steam power. The class was named "Texas" after the Texas & Pacific Railroad, which received the first of the type from the Lima Locomotive Works in 1925. They were designed for use on fast freights along the Pecos Division, better known as the Belen Cutoff between Clovis and Belen. Although five engines were used in California for a brief period, the engines worked most of their lives along this stretch of track. Their home shop was Albuquerque.

While Santa Fe had tested a 2-10-2 with a four-wheel trailing truck in 1919, it wasn't until the late 1920s that the 2-10-4 design was seriously considered by Santa Fe. As freight schedules were reduced to meet competition, speed and power became essential. Purcell was impressed by 2-10-4s being designed for Chesapeake & Ohio, and went ahead with plans for his own. Since the 3751 class 4-8-4s had been a big success, many of their features were incorporated into the new design. The result was prototype engine No. 5000, which was dubbed "Madame Queen" after a radio character on the popular "Amos 'n' Andy" radio show. The new engine, delivered in December 1930 at a cost of $1.33 million, developed 300 pounds of boiler pressure—at the time the highest steam pressure attempted in conventional design. The 5000 was a great success, outperforming 2-10-2s in freight service, and Purcell asked for more. But with the Great Depres-

sion on and tonnage dropping, the Santa Fe board of directors would not approve additional locomotive purchases at the time. Finally, in 1936 the board approved the purchase of new locomotives, including ten 2-10-4s.

It was 1938 before Purcell would get more Texas types. Dubbed the 5001 class, the new engines incorporated several changes from Madame Queen including larger diameter drivers (74-inch versus 69-inch for Madame Queen) and even higher boiler pressure, 310 pounds. Engines 5001-5005, which arrived in June 1938, were coal burners while Nos. 5006-5010, which arrived in July, burned oil. Tenders were identical to those used on the new 3460-class 4-6-4s and 3765-class 4-8-4s, which contributed to the Big Three's family appearance. The new engines were capable of generating more than 6000 hp at speeds above 35 mph. In 1940, the 5001-5005 were converted to oil burners.

While the 2-10-4s gave outstanding service, the arrival of FT diesels from General Motors' Electro-Motive Division in 1941 and their performance convinced the railroad that diesels were the way of the future. However, with the onset of World War II, locomotive production was regulated by the War Production Board, and new FTs were hard to come by. Traffic was on the rise regardless of what locomotives were avail-

able, so in 1943 Santa Fe requested approval for more 4-8-4s (which became the 2900 class) and 25 2-10-4s, which became the 5011 class. The first, 5011, arrived on the property from Baldwin Locomotive Works on June 2, 1944, just four days before D-Day, the Allies' invasion of Europe. The WPB would not allow major changes in design, but the 5011 class all were equipped with roller bearings and carbon steel boilers. The tenders were larger than those carried by the 5001 class, but identical to those used on the 3776 and 2900 class 4-8-4s. They carried 7107 gallons of oil and 24,500 gallons of water. The huge tenders brought the length of the engines to 123 feet, 5 inches. They were the largest steam locomotives built for the Santa Fe. They were also the last.

The 25 engines of the 5011 class were the most powerful two-cylinder steam engines ever constructed, capable of developing 6,500 hp. Equipped with steam lines and signal connections for passenger service, the 5011-series handled troop trains up to 70 mph with ease and would pull regular passenger runs if power was short. After the war ended, the territories worked by the Texas types were extended west to Winslow and east to Waynoka (and sometimes all the way to Wellington, Kansas). Madame Queen and three others were shifted to run

Hudson 3460 wore streamlined shrouding for *Chief* service when that train went lightweight in 1938. Built by Baldwin in 1937, Santa Fe's only fully streamlined steam locomotive wore an unusual robin's egg blue livery which earned it the nickname "Blue Goose." It is shown at Chicago in 1940. *Bud Bulgrin Collection*

Santa Fe had limited success with Mallet-type locomotives, such as 2-6-6-2 No. 3306 at Topeka in 1925. *Bud Bulgrin Collection*

between Albuquerque and La Junta.

Unfortunately, the Texas types were to live short lives on the Santa Fe. In 1944, Fred Gurley became Santa Fe president. He was an early proponent of diesels, dating to his days working at the Burlington when the first *Zephyr* was introduced. Under his tenure the railroad completed dieselization. Diesels took over more and more freight runs in the early 1950s, and an increasing number of 2-10-4s were stored. Their last hurrah came in April and May 1956 when 12 locomotives of the 5011 class were leased to the Pennsylvania Railroad and used between Columbus and Sandusky, Ohio. Placed in coal train service, the 5011s shared tracks with Pennsy's own class J-1 2-10-4s. All were returned and stored by AT&SF in November and December 1956 and never ran again.

The Fall of Steam

The last steam freight run on the Santa Fe occurred on August 4, 1955, when 4-8-4 2912 arrived at Clovis from Slaton, Texas. After that, steam mileage was all in helper service. In 1955 two 2-10-4s were used in helper service over Curtis Hill between Waynoka and Curtis, Oklahoma, but all other steam movements during late 1955, 1956, and 1957 occurred between Belen and Mountainair, New Mexico, with steam locomotives helping diesel-powered trains up the grades of Abo Canyon.

In 1956 only five engines were used,

with total steam mileage at 35,477. The end came for Santa Fe steam in 1957. Five engines, two 4-8-4s and three 2-10-4s, were in operation between June and August. On August 27, 1957, two engines made the final curtain call for steam; 2-10-4 No. 5021 made one last trip out of Belen, helping a diesel-powered train east through Abo Canyon to Mountainair. The locomotive ended its trip back at Belen at 12:20 p.m. The 3780, a 4-8-4, made the same trip that day in helper service between Belen and Mountainair and tied up at Belen at 1:30 p.m. with engineer G. I. Riley and fireman M. E. Key. Santa Fe had owned 3,425 steam engines over the course of its history, and now it was finished after an 88-year reign. Several locomotives were held in reserve storage until 1959, when they were officially written off the books.

The diesel onslaught wiped out not only locomotives, but the servicing facilities and the employees who worked at them. From the 1950s right into the 1980s, roundhouses, shop buildings, coal docks, and other remnants of the steam era fell to the wrecking ball. During steam days there were four overhaul shops on the system: Albuquerque, Cleburne, San Bernardino, and Topeka. The end of steam brought changes to the shops. San Bernardino and Cleburne were converted to handle diesels in 1951, while Topeka overhauled its last steam engine in 1949, then was used only for freight and passenger car overhauls.

CHAPTER 7

The steam shops at Albuquerque, which dated to the days of the Atlantic & Pacific and serviced as many as 29 engines a day in 1929, were closed in 1954 and the erecting shop was reduced to servicing track machinery. By the 1990s Cleburne was closed and the great shops at San Bernardino were demolished, with work switched to Topeka, which once again became a locomotive shop.

Fortunately, the end of regular operations was not the end of the Santa Fe steam story. Both Santa Fe and neighbor Union Pacific possessed farsighted managements, who recognized the accomplishments steam power had made in building their railroads, settling the West, and providing vital service through two world wars. Beginning in the 1950s, Santa Fe began giving away dozens of steam locomotives to communities across its vast system. Just about every division point received a locomotive, as well as dozens of smaller cities. Unlike some railroads, the company saved not only smaller engines, but several examples of the large, modern Big Three. Two locomotives, 4-8-4 2925 and 2-10-4 5021, were held after retirement at the Belen roundhouse, then moved to Albuquerque

when the Belen facility was torn down. Eventually they were donated along with several diesel locomotives to the California State Railroad Museum in Sacramento (in July 1987 the Albuquerque roundhouse was torn down too).

Two Santa Fe steam locomotives have been returned to active service. In addition to the Pacific type in Texas, the company's first 4-8-4, 3751, is back in action. It was placed on display near the San Bernardino passenger depot in 1958. The 3751 held "firsts" in several areas: it was Santa Fe's first 4-8-4, the first 4-8-4 built by Baldwin, and it pulled the first train into the new Los Angeles Union Passenger Terminal in 1939. In 1986, the San Bernardino Railroad Historical Society removed the historic engine from its display site and after an extensive restoration returned the locomotive to service in 1991. The big engine made a special excursion trip from Los Angeles to Bakersfield that year. In 1992 it made a Los Angeles-Chicago round trip, handling an "employee recognition special" for employees and their families. The 3751's occasional trips help bring back fond memories of the wonderful age of Santa Fe steam power.

Northern type locomotives (4-8-4s) were impressive machines on *any* railroad. The 3758 at the head end of a passenger train—possibly one of the *San Diegan* streamliners—about to depart San Diego on February 28, 1946, commanded attention by its sheer girth and large drivers. *Bud Bulgrin Collection*

Impressive is just one of many superlatives that could be applied to the most-modern diesel power found on the Santa Fe during its final years (and on the new BNSF now). Few locomotives are as imposing as a new EMD SD75M or (above) a GE Dash 8-40BW. These machines mean business, and they were members of Santa Fe's "Super Fleet"—the final rein of locomotives that moved Santa Fe trains. *Dan Munson*

At the beginning of the 1930s, the diesel locomotive was an unproven machine. Although several railroads began testing them, and Burlington and Union Pacific began using them in passenger service by mid-decade, by and large diesels had yet to prove their broad range of utility. And then, as is still sometimes the case, railroad management was conservative and resistant to change.

Santa Fe had tried internal-combustion machines before the 1930s. It operated dozens of "doodlebugs," self-propelled rail passenger cars. As early as 1909, Santa Fe acquired a car from the McKeen Company for use on the branch between Chanute and Girard, Kansas. Other cars were purchased from Brill and General Electric, but most came from the then-fledgling Electro-Motive Corporation (EMC), destined to become a leading locomotive manufacturer. Although doodlebugs, which used a gas-distillate engine to provide power for electric traction motors, were successful, they weren't designed for pulling trains; rather, they were low-horsepower machines designed for a specific need—passenger, mail, and express work on lightly patronized branch lines. Some of the cars, rebuilt with new power plants, operated into the 1960s.

The First Diesels

Like many railroads, the first application of diesel locomotion on the Santa Fe was in yard switching service. On February 4, 1935, American Locomotive Company (Alco) delivered a model HH600, No. 2300. The locomotive generated a mere 600 horsepower. The 2300 immediately went to work in the Chicago area and proved more than adequate for the task of handling yard switching chores. Since Santa Fe had a hodgepodge of steam switchers, it welcomed the diesel in yard work. The 2300 remained at work on the AT&SF until it was sold in 1959. From this modest beginning would flow a tide of diesel locomotives that would unseat steam in a mere two decades.

Diesel locomotives first entered road passenger service on the Santa Fe in 1936, then a risky proposition. Burlington had proved the reliability of the diesel power plant in over-the-road service with its *Zephyr* 9900 of 1934. Equipped with a diesel provided by EMC, the *Zephyr* made an incredible nonstop run from Denver to Chicago on May 26, 1934, covering 1,015.4 miles in 13 hours, 4 minutes, and 58 seconds at an average speed of 77.61 mph. However, the *Zephyr* had one distinct disadvantage in the minds of Santa Fe people: it was "articulated"—that is, its passenger-carrying cars were integral to the power car, all being permanently coupled and sharing trucks. Operationally, this prevented the diesel power car from being used on other trains. But if this problem could be overcome, the diesel would have some distinct advantages for the Santa Fe: it could end the need to bring water and coal into the deserts of Arizona and New Mexico for steam locomotives, always a costly practice.

When EMC offered a set of road diesels which could operate independently, Santa Fe took the plunge and ordered two units from EMC. It was a risky decision, considering that diesels had never really been used in the service planned for them by Santa Fe: the transcontinental *Super Chief*.

ABOVE: Santa Fe's early dabblings with internal-combustion power involved distillate-fed motorcars or "doodlebugs." These gas-electrics, as they were also commonly known, became familiar sights on branchlines, hauling mail, express, and perhaps a few adventurous passengers. The M-108 is at Shattuck, Oklahoma, in June 1949, probably serving as trains 39 and 40 on the route to Spearman, Texas. *Bud Bulgrin Collection*

EMC demonstrators 511 and 512 were produced early in 1935 and had the features Santa Fe was seeking: they were non-articulated and generated 1800 hp. Santa Fe ordered two of the boxy units, which arrived in September 1935 as Nos. 1A and 1B. Their carbodies were constructed by St. Louis Car Company and

had cabs on each end of both units. Inside the "twins," as some called them (they were also dubbed "Amos 'n' Andy"), were two 900-hp Winton 201A, V-12 diesel engines. Winton and EMC—both companies were GM subsidiaries—had designed this engine for use in locomotives, but also hoped for contracts from the Navy for submarines.

Testing on the locomotives began shortly after they were delivered on August 30, 1935, and continued until they were placed in regular service in May 1936. The twins had problems: the trailing unit would run hot because of inadequate air-cooling capacity; the steam boilers for heating and air-conditioning the passenger cars were inadequate; and wheels failed and cracked during braking tests. Number 1A even suffered a fire near Gallup on November 20, 1935, and had to be sent back to EMC to be rebuilt, not returning to service until March 1936. But these were pioneering locomotives, the first to be put through such rigorous operating conditions. After the bugs were worked out, they handled the once-a-week round-trip journeys of the new *Super Chief* on its rigorous schedule, hitting speeds as high as 102 mph. Diesel maintainers rode the twins on each trip to ensure their reliability. One of EMC's demonstrator box-cab diesels was also leased as a backup.

By August 1937, Amos 'n' Andy had lost

RIGHT: "Amos 'n' Andy"—originally AT&SF Nos. 1A & 1B (see pages 42-43)—were rebuilt in 1938 into single-ended units and renumbered 1 and 10 respectively. In the process, both received monstrous-looking high cabs and new front truck assemblies. Apparently they could be multipled ("m.u.'ed") with other locomotives, as No. 10 is working with an E1B in this 1945 view near Streator, Illinois. *Bud Bulgrin Collection*

CHAPTER 8

their jobs pulling the *Super Chief* and were placed in the pool of locomotives pulling the *Chief.* In 1938 they were rebuilt with new noses and painted in the red-and-silver passenger livery to put in more years of service. After subsequent rebuildings the two were traded in to EMD during 1953.

Succeeding the twins on the *Super Chief* were a pair of sleek E1 units, E1 No. 2A and cabless booster 2B. ("E" stood for eighteen-hundred horsepower but would come to represent a complete class of locomotive of varying horsepower; after that, the E designation supposedly came to mean "Express.") Like the twins, these new locomotives each contained two 900-hp engines, but beyond that, they were radically different in terms of appearance and construction. These were the first "streamlined" units on the Santa Fe; EMC restyled the front end with a smooth nose, switched from box to truss-carbody construction, and changed from four- to six-wheel trucks to improve high-speed ride quality. The locomotive crew rode up high on these units, affording excellent visibility and safety. Their smooth yet practical design would be the prototype for diesels for years to come.

The 2A and 2B were the first locomotives to wear Santa Fe's now world-famous warbonnet colors, which all newly delivered Santa Fe passenger diesels would wear. Although they missed the first run of the streamlined *Super Chief* due to a traction-motor failure resulting from a pre-inaugural high-speed (36 hours, 49 minutes) L.A.-Chicago run a few days before, the pair did become a big success in *Super*

Chief service. (One of the twins and the leased EMC box-cab diesel demonstrator handled the inaugural *Super Chief* streamliner.)

As the fleet of Santa Fe streamliners grew, the first E1s were followed by orders for more: E1As 3-9 and E1Bs (B stood for "booster" or cabless unit) 3A-4A, delivered in 1937-38. These units turned out to be long-lived: all the E1s were returned to Electro-Motive in 1952 and 1953 for rebuilding into E8Ms with new 2000-hp power plants and new carbodies. Used on secondary passenger runs, the E8Ms remained in service until 1970. In 1938, with more diesels arriving, Santa Fe opened the first diesel shop in the U.S., at 21st Street in Chicago.

The E1s were followed by a new model, E3s 11L and 11A, delivered in 1939. The E3s were a refinement of the E1 model and carried two 1000-hp model 567 V-12 engines. They featured more interchangeable parts produced by EMC rather than General Electric, which had produced many parts for earlier models. There were never any repeat orders for E3s and the pair remained a one-of-a-kind on the Santa Fe roster. However, Santa Fe did buy several refined versions of the E3, the E6 model. The first E6 came in April 1940 followed later by four cab and three booster units.

The first passenger diesels acquired from another builder arrived in May 1941 when Alco delivered 2000-hp DL109 50L and DL-110 50A. Each carried a pair of 1000-hp Alco 539 engines. Although these Alco cabs were unique-looking units with carbodies designed by famous industrial

With their slanted noses, early Electro-Motive E-units were the epitome of sleekness. Witness E6A No. 13 at Kansas City in 1965. Of course, the warbonnet paint and stainless-steel sides help bring such a locomotive's appearance to near perfection. *Mike McBride*

An A-B-B set of Electro-Motive FTs strains upgrade at Houlihan's Curve west of Chilli-cothe, Illinois, with westbound tonnage in 1951. Santa Fe chose Electro-Motive's FT model to began dieselizing in earnest and wound up owning more FTs than any other railroad: 320 out of the 1,096 FTA and FTBs built between 1939 and 1945. In general practice, FTs tended to work in multi-ples of two since by design they were semi-permanently coupled A-B sets, so the appearance of an A-B-B combination here is somewhat uncommon. *R. D. Acton Sr.*

designer Otto Kuhler, they never found wide acceptance and served on only seven railroads. Orphans on the Santa Fe, the pair were scrapped in 1960.

The diesel had gained acceptance in passenger service, and was about to con-quer freight service as well. "The Diesel That Did It" was how *Trains* Magazine termed EMC's famous four-unit set of model FT demonstrators, No. 103, which barnstormed U.S. railroads in 1939-40. Generating 1350 hp each, EMC construct-ed an A-B-B-A (cab-booster-booster-cab) set of the units and turned them loose without fanfare beginning in November 1939. Their mission was to convince rail-roads of the diesel's utility in road-freight service. Over the next 11 months the 103 set rolled 83,764 miles in 35 states. The demonstration worked, and EMD* soon had order books full of requests for FTs. The 103 demonstrator set tested on the Santa Fe from January 2 to February 4, 1940; the railroad was convinced and immediately ordered FTs.

In February 1941 these first production diesels designed for mainline freight service were delivered to Santa Fe. During World War II enough FTs arrived to essentially "dieselize" the main line across the desert between Winslow and Barstow. On this stretch of railroad, "good" water for steam

---

*General Motors had owned EMD since 1930 and formally merged it into the company on January 1, 1941; it became the Electro-Motive Division of General Motors, or simply "EMD."

locomotives had to be hauled in on special "water trains." To help solve this problem, the railroad had increased tender capacity and used chemical treatments for the water. But water-related logistics made the desert the first place to send most new diesels, although steam-powered trains remained on this stretch of line for some time.

Numbered in the 100 series, the FTs wore blue-and-yellow freight colors: Santa Fe was one of a few railroads to adopt one color scheme for its freight locomotives and another for passenger units. Variations of the basic blue-and-yellow garb would con-tinue to adorn freight locomotives until the merger with Burlington Northern. Switch-ers and "road-switchers" wore black paint, or black with silver "zebra stripes" until this was phased out and replaced by the blue and yellow beginning in 1960.

Eventually Santa Fe acquired the largest fleet of FTs of any railroad, 320 units, ini-tially operating in 80 four-unit sets which were broken up in later years. A few FTs even briefly wore warbonnet colors while in passenger service. Santa Fe was anxious to dieselize and expand its premier passenger services but had to wait for new passenger diesel deliveries. As part of its last FT order arriving in 1945, one four-unit set was delivered equipped with steam generators and high-speed gearing for testing in pas-senger service, although it was painted in freight colors. After testing, Santa Fe had ten four-unit FT sets converted to passenger service between April and August 1946. They received 100-mph gearing, steam generators, and the esteemed red-and-silver livery. The FTs initially held down assignments on the *Chief, Super Chief,* and *El Capitan.* Their conversion was not a complete success, as some units suffered traction-motor failures. They were returned to freight service between 1949 and 1952.

Early in the diesel era, the company established the position of diesel maintainer to ease the transition from steam to diesel. The maintainers rode trains across the system, checking equipment, making light repairs, and familiarizing crews with diesels. This evolved into formal training, with school cars making rounds across the railroad. In its last years, the railroad established an instructional facility at Lenexa, Kansas, which included a state-of-the-art locomotive operating simulator. Several railroads contracted with Santa Fe to send their crews to this school.

Dieselization in Full Stride

After World War II ended, diesel purchases continued en masse. In 1946 the railroad received the first of 44 2000-hp PA/PB units from Alco. With their modern lines and six-wheel trucks, the PAs were considered by many the most beautiful diesel locomotive ever designed. They were equipped with a single 2000-hp 16-cylin-der model 244-engine, matching with one engine the horsepower rating of the E3 and E6 models, which carried two engines. Number 51, the first of Santa Fe's PAs, was also Alco's 75,000th locomotive. In celebration of this fact, the locomotive made its debut at the Waldorf-Astoria Hotel in New York City in September 1946. The A-B-A set of PAs were displayed for three days on a siding two floors below the hotel's street level, adjacent to Grand Central Terminal. Although the PAs suffered in later life from high maintenance costs and lack of availability, three of the units were able to develop 5,450 drawbar horsepower at 70 mph while three of their EMD F3 cousins developed only 5,200 drawbar horsepower at the same speed. Santa Fe's were among the last PAs active: most were withdrawn from service in 1968 and officially retired in 1969.

Another one-of-a-kind on Santa Fe's diesel roster was No. 90, a 6000-hp A-B-A set of locomotives built by Fairbanks, Morse & Company, later known as Fairbanks-Morse (F-M). Well known for producing opposed-piston engines for marine use, F-M, based in Beloit, Wisconsin, began producing diesel locomotives in 1944. Santa Fe received its three F-M streamlined units in June 1947. F-M had no model designation for the locomotives, but they were known as "Erie-builts" since they were assembled at the GE plant in

The use of FTs in passenger service was uncommon on most railroads which operated them, but for a relatively short time, Santa Fe did just that. Two, two-unit sets race along with the *Chief* near Streator, Illinois, not too long after the close of World War II. *Bud Bulgrin Collection*

Several railroads widely embraced Fairbanks-Morse power, but on the Santa Fe F-M diesels in over-the-road service were curiosities. Of note was Santa Fe's only passenger FMs, an A-B-A set of "Erie-Builts" (also sometimes known just as "Eries"). Though F-M marketed Eries as dual-service locomotives, Santa Fe painted them in red-and-silver, thus they were at least intended primarily for passenger service on the AT&SF. The threesome are at Chicago's Dearborn Station in April 1949, possibly with the *Grand Canyon. Bud Bulgrin Collection*

Erie, Pennsylvania. GE had been one of F-M's primary suppliers of electrical equipment for its road locomotives. Since F-M was flooded with orders at the end of the war, arrangements were made for GE to assemble FM's streamlined freight and passenger locomotives at Erie. Number 90 had maintenance problems, did not live up to expectations, and was quickly banished from transcontinental passenger runs, handling secondary trains instead. It was traded in to GE on new diesels in 1963.

While the passenger F-M's could be considered a failure, Santa Fe had better luck with F-M switchers and road-switchers. The company obtained three 1000-hp model H10-44 switchers, fifty-nine 1200-hp H12-44 switchers, and twenty 1600-hp H16-44 road-switchers. The railroad even obtained three "special order" F-Ms in 1956: H12-44 switchers on lengthened carbodies and with a short hood to accommodate a steam generator. Santa Fe assigned the units—designated as "H12-44TS'"—to shunt passenger consists in and out of Chicago's Dearborn Station and to switch passenger cars at the nearby 18th Street coach yard. The only units of their kind, they remained in service into the 1970s.

In addition to switch and transfer engines from F-M, Santa Fe obtained diesel switching power from Alco, EMD, and the company which built virtually all modern Santa Fe steam power, the Baldwin Locomotive Works. Even GE, which at the time only built small switchers, furnished nine tiny 44-ton, 380-hp units in 1942-44.

Probably the diesel locomotive most associated with the Santa Fe was the EMD F-unit. With their trademark bulldog nose, four-wheel trucks, and streamlined carbody, Fs were used in both passenger and freight service on railroads across the U.S. After all of Santa Fe's FTs arrived, its next Fs were 1500-hp F3s, delivered beginning in 1946. A modernized, updated version of the FT, Santa Fe acquired 85 of these dependable locomotives for passenger service, with the last arriving in 1949. Even more popular than the F3 was the 1500-hp F7, the best-selling streamlined diesel ever constructed. Santa Fe purchased 326 F7s (although the first eight delivered were technically F3s) for freight service; they were painted blue and yellow and numbered in the 200 class. Another 101 F7s were equipped for passenger service and wore red and silver, with the first coming in September 1949. Of this group, 56 were designated as dual-service models, which could be used interchangeably on passenger or freight runs. Santa Fe's first F7s were built in 1949; the last in 1953. In 1956, late in the F-unit era, more F-units arrived in the form of the F7's successor, the 1750-hp F9. Thirty-six F9s—eighteen

As and 18 Bs—made up Santa Fe's final purchase of F-units. They were assigned to freight service.

Santa Fe had an unusual numbering system for its multiple-unit road diesels such as the F-units, which it began in 1938. Part of this stemmed from the fact that in those days a set of two, three, or four units was treated as a single diesel locomotive and therefore carried but a single number, but with a letter suffix to differentiate between a locomotive's sections. The first locomotive of a multiple-unit set was designated as the lead or "L" unit. The second unit would be designated A, third "B" and so on. For example, a four-unit set of A-B-B-A passenger F3s was designated 16LABC; the trailing "C" also had a cab.

Although F-units certainly looked good heading up trains, Fs in freight service were less than ideal if any switching had to be performed en route. This resulted in the development of the "road-switcher," which had a more utilitarian, box-like appearance that increased visibility and was easier to climb on and off. EMD, Alco, and, beginning in the late 1950s, GE, began producing road-switchers.

Among the most successful of these was the 1500-hp GP7 (GP, for General Purpose; often referred to as "Geeps"). Santa Fe obtained its first model of this type in 1950, and eventually purchased 244 examples, plus five rare GP7 booster units sans cabs. These versatile locomotives worked all across the system and helped finish off steam power. Several were equipped with steam generators so they could work in secondary/branchline passenger service (see Chapter 6). Beginning in 1972 the GP7s were rebuilt, which including "chopping" their high short front hood, new engines, and upgraded electrical systems.

The next member of the Geep family to come aboard was the 1750-hp GP9. Fifty-two examples were received in 1956-57, and like their GP7 sisters, they received the rebuild treatment beginning in 1978. Many examples of rebuilt GP7s/GP9s survived into the 1990s and onto the roster of the Burlington Northern & Santa Fe.

Santa Fe also sampled the road-switchers offered by the Alco, purchasing six 1000-hp RS1s and sixty-three 1600-hp Alco RSD4 and RSD5 road-switchers. The

As the third purchaser of F-M locomotives following F-M's 1945 entrance into the locomotive field, Santa Fe eventually fielded a respectable roster of F-M switchers and a few (20) H16-44-model road-switchers, two of which are with a freight at Topeka in October 1963. *Bud Bulgrin*

Santa Fe seemed to like Alco products. The railroad is often associated with Alco's cherished PA/PB passenger diesels, examples of which can be found in other chapters, but AT&SF had other Alco models as well, including a stable of S-series switchers such as the 2343 working San Bernardino yard in May 1955. *Bud Bulgrin Collection*

Baldwin was a major player in the realm of steam-locomotive construction, but a minority in the diesel era, even on railroads that did make purchases from the Pennsylvania-based builder. Santa Fe's Baldwin diesels were all switchers, two of which are shown at Clovis in 1967. *Tom Hoffmann*

latter were Alco's answer to the Geeps, but with six-wheel trucks which made them sturdy branchline power. Five of the RSD5s came equipped with steam boilers for passenger service.

Two Alco RSD7 demonstrators which packed 2250 hp under their hoods started the railroad on the road to high-horsepower locomotives in 1955. Acquired in April of that year, they had six-wheel trucks and were painted black with silver zebra stripes like the GP7s. After buying the demonstrators, Santa Fe picked up ten more RSD7s, but the production units managed to pull 150 more horsepower out of their 244 engines. Their more successful descendants were the 2400-hp RSD15s which arrived in 1959-60. These locomotives had Alco's newer 251 engine which produced 2400 hp. At the time, they had the longest noses of just about any diesel then in production, and the long snouts earned them the enduring nickname "Alligators." They were delivered in two groups, Nos. 800-823 in 1959 (in black and silver) and Nos. 824-849 in 1960 (blue and yellow). Since they were good luggers, Santa Fe used the RSD15s in heavy-pull situations, such as coal- and ore-train service. After pulling through the 1960s, in 1974 the units were stored and were retired by January 1975. Twelve of them found new homes on other railroads.

Contemporaries of the RSD15s were EMD's SD24 (SD, for <u>S</u>pecial <u>D</u>uty). They were the first EMD-built locomotives to offer an engine that was "turbocharged" for more power, and AT&SF bought 80 examples of the SD24 model. They had the same

horsepower and arrived at the same time as the RSD15s, but outlived their Alco cousins. Alco produced its last locomotive in 1969, and Alco diesels thus became "minority" power on most railroads and often faced early retirement. So, while the RSD15s were being scrapped or sold, the SD24s were being rebuilt in a program begun in 1973 at San Bernardino Shops. Among the improvements they received were new EMD engine assemblies, electrical systems, and traction motors. Dubbed "SD26s," the rebuilds saw several years of continued service before they were scrapped or sold, with a number heading east to New England's Guilford Transportation Industries.

Second-Generation Locomotives

Since steam had been vanquished, EMD concentrated on developing a "second generation" of new power which could be used to replace the aging diesels that had wiped out steam. An early entry in the second-generation EMD catalog was the GP20, which also offered a turbocharged engine, upping engine output to 2000 hp. The arrival of seventy-five GP20s in 1960-61 marked the beginning of the end for the FTs, whose era had begun 20 years earlier. The GP20s initially were used between Kansas City's Argentine Yard and Corwith Yard in Chicago, usually operating in four-unit, 8000-hp combinations. They were equipped with cab signals, necessary for locomotives operating in the lead on the Chicago-Kansas City "Airline." Like just about all the EMD locomotives Santa Fe ordered in the 1960s, the GP20s eventually were remanufactured to extend their service lives; the GP20's were reworked at San Bernardino between 1977 and 1981.

In 1962-63, the GP20s were joined in the Kansas City-Chicago pool by sixteen GE U25Bs, also equipped with cab signals. GE had plunged into the road-locomotive market in 1959 with the U25B, a 2500-hp road-switcher. Within three years GE had captured the Number Two spot in the diesel locomotive market, pushing out Alco.

In 1961, GE sent U25B demonstrators 753-756 onto Santa Fe rails, and the company impressed enough to order sixteen: eight each in 1962 and 1963. The "U" designation referred to GE's "Universal" line, but railroad crews and railroad fans soon began applying the term "U-boat" to U-series diesel—probably to GE's consternation. Santa Fe's new U-boats were frequently used in run-through service with New York Central (Penn Central after February 1968) between Argentine Yard and NYC's big division-point yard at Elkhart, Indiana. Complete trains, including locomotives, were routed between the two roads via a connection at Streator, Illinois. This service, which began in 1967, avoided the congested Chicago terminal.

Introduction of the U25B set off a horsepower war among the locomotive builders. The idea was to produce ever more-powerful locomotives so railroads could replace older units with fewer new ones. For example, EMD marketed its GP20s and the new (1961) 2250-hp GP30 on the basis that three of them could replace four older units. Santa Fe's first GP30s arrived in April 1962, and by June, 35 were on hand. Another order for 50 units brought the total to 85 in 1963. Santa Fe FTs were traded in to the builder on the new units (the GP20s and GP30s all rode on reconditioned trucks of traded FTs), and the last of them left the property in 1966. The GP30 also proved to be long-lived thanks to Santa Fe's rebuild programs.

The GP30 was superseded by the 2500-hp GP35, which was an even more direct response to the U-boat threat posed by GE. It incorporated many design innovations and simplifications offered by the U25B. Santa Fe bought 161 GP35s between 1963 and 1966, and like their GP20 and GP30 sisters, they rode on

trucks from retired FTs; they were rebuilt between 1978 and 1984.

To push horsepower limits ever higher, EMD developed a new prime mover, the 645, which was first offered to customers beginning in 1966 in nine different models. For Santa Fe, the new engine meant it could gain still higher horsepower from fewer units, and in 1966 the company purchased the new SD40 and SD45 models, both of which featured the 645 engine. You could say Santa Fe liked the 3000-hp SD40s, since it bought twenty of them that year—the first SDs since the SD24s in 1960. But the railroad loved the 3600-hp SD45—the world's first 20-cylinder diesel locomotive: it bought 90 units in 1966 and 35 more in 1969-70. Assigned to mainline freights between the Midwest and California/Texas, they were ideally suited to this service, where they could utilize

TOP: Though the red-and-silver "warbonnet" passenger Fs tend to command the spotlight, the freight versions were themselves attractive in the railroad's memorable blue-and-yellow livery. *Jim Boyd*

ABOVE: Briefly during the 1970s, Santa Fe experimented with what became known as its "yellowbonnet" scheme on some passenger Fs, one of which is shown in 1973 on lease to Amtrak. *Mike Schafer*

Electro-Motive enjoyed great success with its GP7/GP9 series road-switchers. "Geeps" were ubiquitous on several major railroads, though to a less extent on Santa Fe, which instead favored F-units. Nonetheless, Santa Fe was one of the few railroads to purchase cabless Geeps. Two GP7s, one cabless, amble along at Sylvester, Texas, with train 119 on February 22, 1969. *Tom Hoffmann*

their power and speed to best advantage.

Santa Fe was still very much a pro-passenger carrier in the 1960s, and by mid-decade its fleet of streamlined E, F, and PA cab units was getting up there in years and mileage. The company turned to GE for new passenger power, and the result was the dual-service (freight/passenger) U28CG of 1966. The 2800-hp, 16-cylinder units—dressed in warbonnet colors of course—were the first new passenger power since the F7s of the 1950s. The U28CGs were really nothing more than a standard U28C road freight locomotive equipped with a steam generator; its non-streamlined boxy design remained.

Santa Fe was happy with its SD45s and other conventional high-horsepower diesels, but it was looking for additional protection for the machinery and for employees that had to use outside walkways on the units while at speed. After years of opting for more boxlike units, the builders went full circle at Santa Fe's behest and designed a non-structural "cowling" for future new hood units. This cowl design also reduced wind resistance and provided for a cleaner engine room.

The first example of the cowl on the

Santa Fe were six GE model U30CGs of 1967. These 3000-hp units were striking in that they carried tall, fluted-steel sides and a wide nose which gave them a distinctive look. Initially, they were assigned to the *Grand Canyon* and San Diego services, but both models were destined to live short lives in passenger service. Following a 1969 passenger train derailment at Chillicothe, Illinois, with two of the U28CGs, all GEs were pulled from passenger service. Eventually they traded their red-and-silver dress code for blue and yellow freight garb.

The most successful of the cowl units were the EMD FP45s, essentially a cowled SD45. The new units had steam generators for train heating, weighed 410,000 pounds, and were 72 feet long. Nine, Nos. 100-108, were delivered to AT&SF in December 1967 and initially were assigned to the *Super Chief/El Capitan*, but the following year they also began working the high-speed *Super C* freight service as well.

These EMD cowl units had long lives. They were withdrawn from passenger service with the advent of Amtrak, painted blue and yellow, then rebuilt in 1980-82 as "SDFP45s." In 1989 eight of the units were repainted in warbonnet colors again and returned to their 100-series numbers to preview new "Super Fleet" freight locomotives. In 1990, the SDFP45s were again renumbered, this time to the 90-series so as not to conflict with new power then arriving.

Santa Fe also amassed a fleet of forty F45-model cowl units in 1968. Although considered freight units, twenty were equipped with steam-line connections so they could be used with FP45s on passenger runs. The F45 was four feet shorter than the FP45 and weighed in at around 390,000 pounds. Like the FPs, Santa Fe remanufactured the F45s in 1982-83, redesignating them "SDF45s" and renumbering them. Most of the F45s remained in service into the 1990s. Six F45's and a single FP45 were sold to new regional railroad Wisconsin Central in 1994-95, and 21 F45s were sold to locomotive remanufacturer/leaser Morrison-Knudsen in 1995.

In 1969-70 more locomotives were added to the fleet. From EMD came 61 2000-hp GP38s for secondary service and 20 2300-hp SD39s. GE produced 49 2250-hp U23Bs; twenty examples of its larger sister, the six-wheeled, 2250-hp U23C; and 25 3300-hp U33Cs. With the cessation of passenger service and the traditional red-and-silver warbonnet passenger paint,

AT&SF beginning in 1972 adapted warbonnet styling to its freight locomotive fleet, but using the blue and yellow. This "yellow bonnet" livery, which even showed up on a few F7s leased to Amtrak, remained in use on freight diesels until the creation of BN&SF. Beginning in 1971, some F7s bumped from passenger service received blue paint on their noses replacing the red, but retained their silver sides.

Santa Fe's most notable rebuilding program also involved its vast fleet of F-units. By 1970 the railroad's huge fleet of F-units was rapidly reaching the end of their economic life. Replacing them with new units would be costly—as would keeping the oldsters on the road. The company turned to its Cleburne shop to remanufacture them. The result was the CF7 (for "Converted F7") program. F7s and F3s would enter the shop and be completely stripped. They were rebuilt as road-switcher units with low, short front hoods, bearing no resemblance to their former, streamlined selves. While not the most attractive locomotives in the world, the CF7s were distinctly Santa Fe, and produced reliable locomotives suited to their service at the fraction of the cost of new power. The first CF7, No. 2649, rolled out on February 27, 1970; the last emerged in 1978 with a total of 132 constructed.

Once Santa Fe had sampled second-generation diesel power through the SD24 and GP20 purchases of the late 1950s and early 1960s, it was off to the races for other new second-generation locomotives. On this westbound at Joliet during the famous Chicagoland "Blizzard of '67," EMD GP30s and GE U25Bs give a new look to freights on the Chicago-Kansas City "Airline." For part of the 1960s on this main line, GP20s were the ruling locomotive. *Mike Schafer*

RIGHT: With its V-20 prime mover, EMD's SD45/SD45-2 model was a stand-alone in dieseldom. A number of roads sampled it, but Santa Fe was one of the few that really took a strong fancy to the 3600-hp locomotives, buying over 200 of both the regular and "Dash 2" models. Flared radiators make the SD45s easy to spot in a crowd. Grimy-but-new 1806 is at Kansas City in 1966. *Jim Boyd*

BELOW: Utilitarian was in and streamlining was out on the GE U28CG passenger diesels of 1966, but the warbonnet scheme still gave these units a classy look at the head end of passenger trains. They were used quite a bit on the Texas Chief, shown blazing out of Chicago in the summer of 1967. Only Santa Fe owned U28CGs—ten of them. *George Speir*

After years of service on the Santa Fe, dozens of CF7s were resold to short line and industrial railroads across the country. If longevity is the measure, then the CF7 program is probably the most successful locomotive rebuild ever.

The 1970s brought another round of large diesel purchases. By 1972 EMD was in the enviable position of having captured 80% of the domestic locomotive market, and rather than making wholesale changes to its line, concentrated on improving it. The result was the "Dash 2" whose highlight was a modular electrical cabinet: if a system failed, the module would simply be replaced. There were also other internal changes such as new pistons and liners in the engine.

Railroads, including Santa Fe, quickly accepted the design changes, and the railroad was the first owner of the SD45-2, accepting 90 units. Then, Santa Fe switched its allegiance to the SD40-2, which was less expensive to maintain than the V-20 SD45 series, purchasing 197 SD40-2s in six groups between 1977 and 1981. The SD40-2 turned out to be EMD's most successful product since the F-unit. But Santa Fe, with considerable investment in SD45s, did not abandon that model; instead it

rebuilt them during the 1980s. By the 1990s new power had displaced many of them, and 55 of the older SD45s were sold to Wisconsin Central.

As the railroad was buying EMD products, it was also keeping GE busy. In the high-horsepower category, Santa Fe had purchased the SD45's competing model, the 3600-hp U36C. One hundred were delivered between 1972 and 1975. Beginning in 1985, 70 of these locomotives were remanufactured at Cleburne and redesignated "SF30C's." They were the only GEs rebuilt.

Competing with the SD40-2, GE's C30-7 was another popular locomotive, and Santa Fe bought 157 of that model. Smaller, four-axle GEs arrived on the property in the form of 69 B23-7s, which came in four orders between 1978 and 1984, and sixteen B36-7s which came in 1980. The "B-boats" were successors to the Universal series as GE began its run at Number One builder EMD.

Other locomotives received during this period included 106 of EMD's 2300-hp GP39-2, for mainline, local, and yard service. In 1978, ten 3500-hp "GP40Xs" from EMD. These were testbed locomotives, a preview of EMD's "Super Series" locomotives of the 1980s which introduced com-

puterization to locomotive technology. They had new computerized wheel-slip control to increase tractive effort and new 16-645F3 engines. After the GP40Xs, Santa Fe's next Super Series locomotives were a group of 45 GP50s. Essentially regular production versions of the GP40X, the 3500-hp GP50s came in two groups: thirty in 1981 and fifteen in 1985.

Eighteen more cowl units came to the Santa Fe in 1984 when it traded forty-three older locomotives to Amtrak for eighteen SDP40F models—basically cowled SD40-2s. Amtrak intended them to be its locomotive of the future when they first came on line in 1973, but derailments involving the units led to their being banned by several Amtrak host railroads even though it could never be proven the units were at fault. Santa Fe never had any problems with them, and after acquiring them they were rebuilt at San Bernardino, emerging as "SDP40F-2s."

Third-Generation Diesel Power

The mid-1980s saw more changes coming to the locomotive fleet. The two locomotive builders were introducing more computer technology, and horsepower ratings were creeping up. During 1988-89

Both GE and EMD had strong showings on the Santa Fe during the second-generation diesel era. At Joliet, Illinois, in 1977, a GP39-2 on a local holds back while a westbound through freight led by a GE U36C (and including some Canadian National power) rattles the bricks in the platform of Union Station. *Steve Smedley*

AT&SF's CF7 rebuild program was enormously successful (except, some locomotive aficionados would argue, in the esthetics department). One hundred thirty-two F-units were reincarnated as CF7s during the 1970s program, and many were still active on shortlines throughout the country as the century drew to a close. The 2571 is at Riverside, California, in 1982. *Steve Glischinski*

more EMD Super Series came on line, this time forty 3800-hp GP60s. GE also delivered forty examples of its new Dash 8-40Bs, which developed 4,000 horsepower.

As the Eighties wore on, Santa Fe was about to lead the way in revolutionizing motive-power design. In 1988, Santa Fe officials and employees examined ways to improve locomotive cabs. A Cab Redesign Committee was formed to concentrate on improving cab comfort and safety. The Committee took a close look at Canada, where Canadian National had been using wide-nose "comfort" cabs for many years. In addition to creature comforts, the cabs were designed to better withstand impact in collisions. Santa Fe even borrowed a CN locomotive to study the cab and its desktop-type control console.

The result of this study was the production of locomotives with new, wide-nose comfort cabs incorporating ergonomically designed seats, thick insulation, and desktop controls. The first locomotive delivered with the "North American Safety Cab" was UP SD60M 6085, released on January 10, 1989. Since that time, virtually all of the new high-horsepower locomotives produced have been built with the safety-cab design.

At the same time the new cab design was being conceived, Michael R. Haverty became president of the Santa Fe. His administration revived the classic red-and-silver warbonnet passenger colors (see Chapter 5), applying them to the next order of new locomotives from EMD and GE as well as to the 100-series FP45s which in their "new" colors first hit the rails in late summer 1989.

In early 1990 the first new power to carry the warbonnet and the new cab design arrived in the form of 63 EMD GP60Ms. Numbered in the 100-series, their arrival forced the FP45s to be renumbered once again, back to the 90-series. Later in the year 60 GE Dash 8-40BWs arrived, Nos. 500-559. Both locomotive classes were immediately assigned to high speed, long-distance intermodal service. Clad in the red and silver, the new locomotives were dubbed the "Super Fleet," capitalizing on the days of the *Super Chief* and *Super C*.

In 1991 a return to booster units occurred when the railroad received 23 GP60Bs. When these cabless engines arrived, it was a case of "back to the future" along Santa Fe lines: you could again stand trackside and watch a matched set of A-B-B-A locomotives roar by. The GP60Bs would be the last EMD products Santa Fe would purchase for four years. After making a considerable investment in new paint for Super Fleet locomotives, the company in 1992 opened a brand new wash rack at Corwith Yard in Chicago to keep grime off the new locomotives.

With the arrival of the Super Fleet came new agreements with the builders for maintaining them. In 1989 the railroad reached an agreement with GE under which that company agreed to assume responsibility for maintenance of the railroad's GE fleet. GE had guaranteed performance and reliability goals it had to meet,

and the railroad agreed to pay a prescribed fee based on mileage operated by the units, commonly called a "power-by-the-mile" agreement. GE agreed to provide technical advisors to supervise maintenance work by Santa Fe shop workers at the Argentine Yard locomotive facility in Kansas City; GE would reimburse the railroad for labor expenses. The new agreement cut costs by reducing labor costs and the necessity of maintaining parts inventories. In January 1990 Santa Fe reached a similar agreement with General Motors, with EMD technicians based at the locomotive facilities at Corwith Yard in Chicago. In 1994 another agreement was reached with Morrison-Knudsen to maintain 278 EMD locomotives at Barstow and Argentine, with Santa Fe paying for the use of the units by the mile.

Satisfied with the performance and the quick delivery schedules afforded by General Electric, Santa Fe in its final years flooded Erie with orders for Super Fleet locomotives. In 1992, 23 more Dash 8-40BWs (560-582) and 67 Dash 8-40CWs (800-866) arrived. These 3800-hp locomotives were Santa Fe's first six-axle power since 1983. Sticking with six-axle Warbonnets, 1993 saw the arrival of Dash 8-40CWs with 4,135 horsepower (GE

classified them Dash 8-41CWs). A total of 85 of the monster GEs arrived that year, numbered 867-951, with the last arriving in November 1993.

In early 1994 Santa Fe received the latest design in GE's "Dash" series when it ordered 50 Dash 9-44CWs, numbered 600-649. These locomotives featured a new style of six-axle high-adhesion trucks, which had traction motors that all faced the same direction to deliver more power to the rail. A second order for Dash 9s, Nos. 650-699, arrived in the last half of 1994.

Late in 1994 Santa Fe returned to EMD with an order for 25 SD75Ms for delivery in 1995, and later opted for 26 more. This later order included an option for yet another 25 locomotives. The SD75Ms would be the last new locomotives received by Santa Fe.

The SD75M incorporated a 16-cylinder 710G prime mover generating 4,300 horsepower, with the last five units of the order experimentally upgraded to 4500 hp. They weighed 394,000 pounds, exerted 109,000 pounds of tractive effort, and carried 5,000 gallons of fuel. Contrast this with Amos 'n' Andy of 1935, which each carried two 900-hp engines and two 400-gallon fuel tanks. The SD75Ms were numbered 200-250, with the first arriving on March 29, 1995,

Modern, third-generation power on the Santa Fe is well illustrated in this panorama of an A-B-B-A combination of GP60s sweeping through the deserts of New Mexico near Laguna in 1995. Several other illustrated examples of third-generation motive power discussed in this chapter can be seen in Chapter 5. *Steve Glischinski*

and the last, No. 250, arriving on September 4, 1995. The option to purchase 25 more SD75Ms was exercised, but by the time they arrived the BN and AT&SF holding companies had merged. These new units carried BNSF lettering on their long hoods and were numbered 8251-8275, although the Santa Fe wrap-around nose emblem was retained.

By the time of the merger, more warbonnetted locomotives were on the rails at one time than ever before, even in the glory days of passenger service. By September 1995, 475 diesels wore the colors (five Super Fleet units, including one FP45, had been wrecked and scrapped since 1989). BN&SF indicated it would retain the colors, but with BNSF lettering. Even after the holding companies merged, several locomotives continued to be painted in Santa Fe blue and yellow. But it was left to SD75M No. 250—the last new locomotive delivered in complete Santa Fe paint and markings—to lower the curtain on 60 years of Santa Fe diesel history.

However, Santa Fe diesel history will live on, even after the last Santa Fe diesel is repainted. Thanks to Santa Fe employees R. E. McMillan and Joe McMillan (not related), AT&SF was one of the few railroads to have an active program of preserving internal-combustion locomotives, which began in 1972 when R. E. McMillan was assistant to Santa Fe's Vice President–Operations. At Belen and later Albuquerque, the company saved several examples of diesel power, which shared roundhouse space with a rare 1932 self-propelled motorcar and the 4-8-4 and 2-10-4 which were held for preservation at the end of the steam era. Through the advice of Joe McMillan, Santa Fe carefully selected examples of rare diesel power and moved them to storage at the Albuquerque shop. Although a Santa Fe museum had been proposed, the idea never came to fruition. Instead, on the eve of the aborted Santa Fe-Southern Pacific merger in 1986, the entire collection was donated to the California State Railroad Museum in Sacramento. At this writing most of the collection is in storage in Sacramento where they await an undetermined future.

The new Burlington Northern & Santa Fe Railway has also shown a knack for diesel preservation. In 1997, the company donated one of the FP45s—one of only fourteen built—to the Illinois Railway Museum at Union, Illinois, near Chicago. The museum also displays former Santa Fe 2407, an RSD15 which after retirement had been sold to the Lake Superior & Ishpeming. Also on hand is 4-8-4 2903, which was moved from the Museum of Science & Industry in Chicago.

Four Santa Fe Alco PA-type locomotives were sold to the Delaware & Hudson Railway in 1967, and all ultimately ended up in Mexico. Two have been preserved in Mexican museums, and the other two are the subject of an effort by private individuals and the Smithsonian Institution to return them to the U.S. for preservation. If these efforts bear fruit, it may once again be possible to see one of the most handsome diesels ever constructed, wearing the most famous diesel paint scheme of all time, rolling down the high iron again.

Last but not least . . . Santa Fe diesel history closed out with the purchase of SD75Ms from Electro-Motive—the last units delivered in Santa Fe livery and lettering. The 216 is making time for Chicago in June 1996 at Monica, Illinois. *Mike Schafer*

CHAPTER 8

Appendix

STEAM LOCOMOTIVES

No.	Type	Location
1	2-8-0	*Cyrus K. Holliday*, to Kansas State Historical Society
5	0-4-0	California State Railroad Museum, Sacramento
643	2-8-0	State Fairgrounds, Oklahoma City
664	2-8-0	Travel Town, Griffith Park, Los Angeles
735	2-8-0	State Fairgrounds, Hutchinson, Kansas
761	2-8-0	Stone Park, Wickenburg, Arizona
762	2-8-0	Santa Fe Park, Chanute, Kansas
769	2-8-0	Old Coal Mine Museum, Madrid, New Mexico
811	2-8-0	At Union Station, Atchison, Kansas
870	2-8-0	Old Coal Mine Museum, Madrid, New Mexico
940	2-10-2	Johnstone Park, Bartlesville, Oklahoma
1010	2-6-2	California State Railroad Museum, Sacramento
1015	2-6-2	Fremont Park, Emporia, Kansas
1024	2-6-2	West First St., La Junta, Colorado
1050	2-6-2	Riverside Park, Independence, Kansas
1057	2-6-2	Sellers Park, Wellington, Kansas
1073	2-6-2	Central Park, Lawrence, Kansas
1079	2-6-2	Walter Johnson Park, Coffeyville, Kansas
1080	2-6-2	City Park, Brownwood, Texas
1096	2-6-2	Children's Home Park, Blackwell, Okla.
1108	2-6-2	City Park, Ardmore, Oklahoma
1129	2-6-2	City Park, Las Vegas, New Mexico
1139	2-6-2	Boot Hill Museum, Dodge City, Kansas
1316	4-6-2	Texas State Railroad, Rusk, Texas (operational, now numbered 500)
1809	2-6-2	City Park, Slaton, Texas
1819	2-6-2	City Park, Lamar, Colorado
1880	2-6-2	Military Park, Newton, Kansas
1951	2-8-0	Wacker Park, Pauls Valley, Oklahoma
2522	2-8-0	City Park, Fairview, Oklahoma
2542	2-8-0	Wilson Park, Arkansas City, Kansas
2546	2-8-0	Walt Disney Park, Marceline, Missouri
2903	4-8-4	Illinois Railway Museum, Union, Illinois
2912	4-8-4	Union Station, Pueblo, Colorado; may be restored.
2913	4-8-4	Riverview Park, Fort Madison, Iowa
2921	4-8-4	Beard Brook Park, Modesto, California
2925	4-8-4	California State Railroad Museum, Sacramento
2926	4-8-4	Coronado Park, Albuquerque, New Mexico
3415	4-6-2	Eisenhower Park, Abilene, Kansas
3416	4-6-2	City Park, Great Bend, Kansas
3417	4-6-2	City Park, Cleburne, Texas
3423	4-6-2	Railroad & Pioneer Museum, Temple, Texas
3424	4-6-2	Highway Park, Kinsley, Kansas
3450	4-6-4	LA County Fairgrounds, Pomona, California
3463	4-6-4	Fairgrounds, Topeka, Kansas
3751	4-8-4	Operational, stored in Riverside, California
3759	4-8-4	City Park, Kingman, Arizona
3768	4-8-4	AT&SF Depot, Wichita, Kansas
5000	2-10-4	Santa Fe Park, Amarillo, Texas
5011	2-10-4	Museum of Transportation, St. Louis, Missouri
5017	2-10-4	National Railroad Museum, Green Bay, Wisconsin
5021	2-10-4	California State Railroad Museum, Sacramento
5030	2-10-4	City Park, Santa Fe, New Mexico
9005	0-6-0	Hillcrest Park, Clovis, New Mexico

DIESEL LOCOMOTIVES

No.	Type	Location
17	PA1	Federal Electric Commission Museum, Mexico City (ex-Santa Fe 60L)
19	PA1	Nacional de los Ferrocarriles (National Railroad Museum), Puebla, Mexico (ex-Santa Fe 66L)
92	FP45	Illinois Railway Museum, Union, Illinois
M160	Motorcar	Age of Steam Railroad Museum, Dallas, Texas
M177	Motorcar	Travel Town, Griffith Park, Los Angeles
M190	Motorcar	California State Railroad Museum, Sacramento
347C	F7A	California State Railroad Museum, Sacramento
347B	F3B	California State Railroad Museum, Sacramento
543	H12-44TS	State Railroad Museum, Sacramento
608	H12-44	California State Railroad Museum, Sacramento
2260	DS4-4-10	California State Railroad Museum, Sacramento
2301	SC600	Railroad & Pioneer Museum, Temple, Texas
2381	S2	California State Railroad Museum, Sacramento
2394	RS1	California State Railroad Museum, Sacramento
2404	NW2	California State Railroad Museum, Sacramento
LS&I 2407	RSD15	Illinois Railway Museum, Union, Illinois (ex-Santa Fe 9841/841)
9820	RSD15	California State Railroad Museum, Sacramento
9823	RSD15	Promontory Chapter, National Railway Historical Society, Salt Lake City, Utah (ex-Santa Fe 823)

Index